How Does America Hear the Gospel?

HOW DOES
AMERICA
HEAR
THE GOSPEL?

William A. Dyrness

WILLIAM B. EERDMANS PUBLISHING COMPANY
GRAND RAPIDS, MICHIGAN

Copyright © 1989 by Wm. B. Eerdmans Publishing Co.
255 Jefferson Ave. S.E., Grand Rapids, Mich. 49503

Printed in the United States of America

Library of Congress Cataloging-in-Publication Data

Dyrness, William A.
   How does America hear the gospel? / William A. Dyrness.
     p.   cm.
   Includes bibliographical references.
   ISBN 0-8028-0437-3
   1. United States—Church history—20th century. 2. United States—
Religion—1960–   . 3. Christianity and culture. I. Title.
BR526.D97   1989
261'.0973—dc20   89-39253
                                                 CIP

To my children Michelle, Andrea, and Jonathan,
who have taught me to see the joy and pain
of being American.

CONTENTS

CONTENTS

CONTENTS

PREFACE

TO MAKE MEANINGFUL GENERALIZATIONS ABOUT AMERICAN culture is virtually impossible. This obvious fact does not keep people from trying; indeed, every American must at various times generalize to make sense of her experience. This book is a species of that generic foolishness. However difficult self-definition may be, it seems even more foolish to deny that living in America at the end of the 20th century has enormous implications for what we hear God saying to us in Scripture. Our context necessarily provides the forms that clarify and distort our reception of the gospel.

I write as a theologian who has learned a great deal from historians and sociologists, and yet cannot claim special competence in these fields. But this discussion among the disciplines is very important for all of us who seek to follow Christ at this point in history. And though I think what I say is important for theologians, I am by no means writing only for them. I mean to address all who call themselves Christian and have felt the tension between the values of Christianity and those of American culture. Moreover, my purpose is not simply to help us understand our context better, but to encourage us to be better servants of the Christ we claim to follow. For true understanding grows out of an obedient involvement in God's work of reconciling the world to himself.

This discussion has benefited from many friends who have taken the time to listen to the argument, either in oral or written form.

My students at New College Berkeley and those in the 1987 Summer School of Fuller Theological Seminary were the first to try to make sense of these ideas in my course "Theology in America." Ken Morris, my research assistant while I wrote the manuscript, Ruth Sill, and Douglas Firth Anderson have been a special help, and continue to suggest more bibliography than I can possibly read. Colleagues Robert K. Johnston, James W. McClendon, Jr., Richard Mouw, Mark Noll, and Joel Green have proven their friendship by reading all or part of the manuscript and making many valuable comments.

Parts of the book were given as lectures at Denver Theological Seminary and at Mennonite Brethren Biblical Seminary in Fresno. I would like to thank the faculty and students of these schools and especially Haddon Robinson at Denver and Howard Loewen in Fresno for their hospitality. Part of Chapter Two appeared in *The Reformed Journal*, to whom I am grateful for permission to reprint.

With all this help the book ought to be better than it is, but it is sent forth with the prayer that many others will be encouraged (or provoked) by it to join the conversation about how we in America will together "grow up in every way into him who is the head, into Christ" (Eph. 4:15).

Berkeley, California
July 1988

CHAPTER ONE

Introduction:
In Search of Theological Roots

SINCE THE APPROACH TO ISSUES DISCUSSED IN THIS BOOK HAS come about through unusual circumstances, I begin the study with some personal remarks. In short, these chapters are my initial attempt to sort out the ways in which our personal and cultural setting affects the way we act and think as Christians. What difference does it make to my understanding of Christianity that I have been raised in the suburban Midwest of the United States, while, for example, some of my students have been raised in remote islands of the Philippines?

Reflections on Theological Education
in Asia and America

Growing up in the church, I was not encouraged to ask questions like this. Nor did my theological education encourage such questions. I was raised in an evangelical Bible church in suburban Chicago. My theological education was, by most Western standards, fairly typical and adequate—a B.A. in philosophy, a B.D. in theology, followed by three years

1

of graduate study in Europe. Though I studied in culturally diverse settings—Georgia, California, France—this did not affect the fact that I studied within and interacted with a single intellectual tradition. Since I completed my formal education, a great many things have changed the way theology is taught, but the monocultural assumptions that dominate Western thinking about Christianity remain largely unchallenged.

Even during my first years of pastoring in Portland, Oregon, I became aware of vast worlds of experience with which I had had no contact. I remember sitting in an untidy apartment, calling on a visitor to my church. A baby was screaming and the television blaring, while I feebly sought to communicate some kind of concern. What shape could I give my witness that would penetrate this world?

After three years' experience as a pastor, I went to teach theology in the Philippines. My training and experience had conditioned me to feel that our particular historical and cultural setting, while important, was clearly secondary to the truth contained in the Bible and defended in evangelical theology texts. If our context determines what we find in the Bible, I would have argued, everyone will be doing theology differently and there will be no standard of truth.

But I very soon saw that even the detached way I phrased this question reflected a Western point of view. Moreover, I soon saw that my questions had little relevance to the students I was teaching. My questions went along these lines: How do I know the Bible is true? What is the nature of authority? How do I conceptualize God? My students' questions were very different and included the following: Why are so many of our people poor? (One student even dared to pass me a note after class asking: Why do missionaries live in large houses when their national colleagues struggle to make ends meet and live crowded in small apartments?) What does the Bible have to say about suffering? Oppression? Justice? The spirits?

In evangelism these differences were equally evident. I

had been taught to deal with issues of personal identity and meaning. My students had little sympathy for our Western "identity crises." They wanted to solve much more practical issues of food, jobs, and health care. I still remember the puzzlement with which my friends greeted Francis Schaeffer's discussion of Western (and European) existential issues. One of the first campus groups which asked me to speak was facing a major challenge: how would they respond to leftist groups around them which confronted the martial law government of Philippine President Ferdinand Marcos with concrete social programs? What social program did the Bible suggest? My tendency to focus on issues of personal meaning (what I was taught to call "spiritual concerns") somehow did not seem appropriate to the urgency of their situation.

As I scurried about to find something to say to these friends, I realized that as far as I could remember I had never preached or taught on issues of wealth and poverty—I certainly had no category for it in my files. Now I was gradually being exposed to these issues, though I would never feel them as my students did. As puzzling as my own context, these issues struck with a power and immediacy I hadn't known before.

In the morning my walk to the bus took me by a squatter community along the banks of a winding stream. And my wife began a graduate program in urban anthropology in which we together learned about the underground economy, marginal workers, and government relocation programs.

These issues came to a head for me the year we offered a special Master of Theology program in our seminary, focused entirely on a biblical theology of wealth and poverty. This was designed for students from throughout Asia who wanted advanced training that was relevant to their Asian setting. For nine months teachers and students read and pondered Scripture and theology together and learned from each other. We began to understand that everyone is poor in one way or another and that God wants to use our various poverties as a way of showing his love. For my students, poverty was often associated with disease and hunger; for us in the West poverty often had to do with ennui and an indigence of relationships. Moreover, where one was weak, the other tended to be strong, making it conceivable that there could be real sharing in the body of Christ.

Of course, my Western background and education were not simply a handicap; they also gave me an important perspective that contributed to the conversation. And my students' background resulted in their own blindspots: their propensity for concrete thinking sometimes made it difficult for them to put their problems into a larger (abstract!) framework. Their desire for harmony and consensus sometimes impaired their ability to be critical of one another's ideas.

But through this program a genuine interaction between traditions began to take place. As I helped my students develop critical tools for their work, they helped me see ways in which my own cultural background had influenced my thinking. Their questions became a vehicle by which all of us together learned something from Scripture that we had not seen before. The resulting dialogue about God's purposes and the meaning of "salvation" was greatly enriched, and we were all more excited than ever about what God was doing among us.

Our theological reflection consisted first in a careful reexamination of Scripture in the light of our situation. As we grew more conversant with biblical theology, a field that has grown worldwide in our century, we became aware of the centrality of God's response to human suffering and pain. We saw that God's mission of delivering his people, what we call "redemption," is central to the biblical account, and ought to be central for us. We noticed that in the New Testament theological reflection is almost always related to communicating and extending the gospel. Theology in the New

INTRODUCTION: IN SEARCH OF THEOLOGICAL ROOTS

Testament is virtually a theology of mission, and this is what
gives it its dynamic, vital quality. But this also brought it into
immediate relation to the economic and religious issues of
that day. Questions about idolatry, the poor, and the role of
women (and widows) are central New Testament concerns.

After three years of ministry in North America and this
new experience in Asia, I began to suspect that the study of
theology in the West was several steps removed from
people's lives. This feeling has been corroborated by several
recent studies on theological education in America. Theologian Edward Farley, for example, has lamented that theology
has lost its connection with actual life and has been dispersed
into several "sciences" in which theory and practice are
alienated. These sciences are not without importance, but
their integration with issues of practical discipleship is often
unclear. Theology, he concludes, is now for ministers, not for
human beings (*Theologia*, 134). Small wonder theology often
evokes the kind of response I received at a party from a
Harvard-trained specialist in international development.
When I informed him that I taught theology, he quipped:
"Theology! Now there's a conversation stopper!"

Historian Bruce Kuklick has recently illuminated the
process by which theological education has become "profes-
sionalized" in North America. His assessment is worth quot-
ing at length:

> By the 1830s, after the first flush of enthusiasm for the New
> Haven Theology, debate in New England had relinquished
> none of its rigor but much of its appeal. Religious thinkers
> did not lose the sanction of their legitimating communi-
> ties, but they did lose their interest. In the first American
> ivory towers, the divines catered more and more to ad-
> vanced ministerial students and said little to people out-
> side graduate classrooms. Often contemptuous of changes
> in European thought and unmoved by the need to diver-
> sify their ranks, theologians lost vigor. (*Churchmen and
> Philosophers*, 118)

As a result, what in our seminaries we call theology is more often reflection on previous thinking than biblically-informed reflection on life. We spend more time learning what other people thought about theology and how still others responded to them than about how we may respond obediently to the issues that face us. One would be unwise to make a strict dichotomy between these two, since both are obviously part of the theological task and important to the church. Indeed, one might generalize and say that Third World theology often neglects sustained reflection because of the pressing demands of life, while our educational programs are clearly weighted in the direction of specialized and abstract thinking to the neglect of these demands.

A sure symptom of this problem is the way missions and evangelism are tacked on in courses at the end of our study of systematic theology, rather than occupying the central place they do in Scripture. The resulting alienation between theology and evangelism (and between theologians and evangelists!) has done much to sap the vitality from both our theology and our evangelism. As we will see in our study of Robert Schuller, while evangelists have often been more contextually oriented, they have not had the critical collaboration of theologians. Meanwhile, to borrow the language of missiology, theology has become contextualized to its religious subculture, most recently to its place in the academic guild, rather than to its broader life setting (see Dyrness, "The Contribution of Theological Studies").

I intend to say no more about the weaknesses (or strengths) of theology in America, though what we discuss has important implications for both. Indeed, my concern is with the way American Christians in general might be encouraged to understand and appropriate their setting. While in Asia, we became convinced of the need to begin our reading of Scripture, and thus our reflection on Christianity, in the light of Asian culture. The parallel questions we face here are these: what are the questions which motivate people in North America? How might we begin a fresh reading of Scripture here?

Theology and Culture

Before taking up these questions, we may fairly ask what we mean by theology and culture in this discussion. "Theology" is the way a particular community of people speaks of God and his work in the light of its particular cultural and historical reading of Scripture. A premise of this study is that repentance and the response of faithful obedience are the condition, not the result, of theology. Theology is reflection upon the movement of mission that is already in process when a person or group responds to Jesus Christ (see Daniel Van Allmen, 1975). The shape of this response will reflect the particularities of the setting, and the subsequent reading of Scripture will reflect back critically on that setting. Notice that on this view of things mission—God's redemptive work and our involvement in that process—provides the central dynamic for theological reflection, just as it does in the New Testament.

By "culture" we refer to all the learned behavior and symbols that make our world home. Clyde Kluckhohn describes culture more fully as follows:

> Culture consists of patterns, explicit and implicit, of and for behavior acquired and transmitted by symbols, constituting the distinctive achievement of human groups, including their embodiments in artifacts: the essential core of culture consists of traditional (i.e., historically derived and selected) ideas and especially their attached values; culture systems may, on the one hand, be considered as products of action, on the other as conditioning influences upon further action. (In Malina, *The New Testament World*, 11)

Notice that ideas and attitudes as well as symbols and artifacts make up the meaning by which we live. This is

7

important for the Christian because we believe that the early chapters of Genesis portray people as created for culture. Adam and Eve are told to name and have dominion over the created order as they live out their lives in the presence of one another and God. In fact, it seems that a substantial part of their response to God consisted in their development of culture.

This dimension of life is important for us for a second reason. Just as the Fall distorted our attempts to build a world of meaning, so salvation must have the result of renewing cultural life as well as individuals. Just as sin inevitably had its impact on culture, so forgiveness and the new creation will impact wider cultural values (I discuss this more fully in *Let the Earth Rejoice*).

Two further implications for our Christian living and thinking flow from this definition of culture. First, the fact that people are left free by God in a material world to create their own environment indicates that each "world" people create—each separate culture—is to be treated with a special dignity. This is the theological equivalent of the axiom anthropologists call cultural relativity. That is, each people is to be understood on its own terms; no single people will develop values that can judge any other. Not that all the values people develop are equally good or true. But they first must be understood in their setting. All values will display particular strengths and weaknesses when judged by the standard of God's Word. But these judgments must always be made in context.

A second corollary follows from this. Just as salvation has special implications for culture, so each culture has its own particular contribution to make to our Christian maturity. Ephesians 4:13 looks forward to the day when "we all attain to the unity of the faith and of the knowledge of the Son of God." This is clearly a corporate achievement in which Christians from every culture will play a role. So John envisions the final gathering of the redeemed in heaven in this way:

> After this I looked, and behold, a great multitude which
> no man could number, from every nation, from all tribes
> and peoples and tongues, standing before the throne and
> before the Lamb, clothed in white robes, ... and crying out
> with a loud voice: "Salvation belongs to our God who sits
> upon the throne, and to the Lamb!" (Rev. 7:9, 10)

A focus on cultural values has limitations which must
be recognized at the outset. Such a study must be supple-
mented by a careful study of political and structural factors
on the one hand, and by intellectual factors on the other. For
the former one might consult John Coleman and Max Stackhouse; for the latter Allan Bloom and Lesslie Newbigin are
helpful guides. But there is an important justification for this
particular concentration. American Christians do not primarily define their faith in intellectual, but pragmatic terms.
Their Christian understanding grows out of the dynamics of
life. As Edward Farley put it: "The dialectic of theological
understanding is set in motion here, by the matters which
evoke response and interpretation" (165). For Americans this
dialectic consists in important cultural factors: deep-seated
expectations, a unique cultural history, and a special relation
to their environment. It is hardly debatable that some of the
most important battles of our generation are being fought on
the level of cultural values, factors reflected more readily in
our arts and literature than in our theological texts.

In this study we will apply these questions to our own
North American setting. How can we describe the process by
which the American middle class tends to hear and construe
the gospel? What are the major concerns reflected in this
process? Pursuing this agenda will provide important
materials for a discipleship (and eventually a theology) that
is potentially both biblical and American.

CHAPTER TWO

How Does America Hear the Gospel?

IN HIS ALASKAN TRAVELS JOHN MUIR CAME ACROSS AN Indian tribe that had eagerly accepted Christianity. When Muir inquired as to why they had been so receptive, he was told a fascinating story. About twenty or thirty years earlier there had been a particularly bitter war with a neighboring tribe. The battles never ended because each victory brought a fresh retaliation; the scores were never settled.

After an unusually difficult summer of fighting, this tribe sent a delegation to its neighbors. "Look," they said, "winter will soon be here and we have had no time to gather our food. We are all facing starvation if we do not stop our fighting."

"We cannot stop," the neighbors responded. "You have killed ten more men than we have; give us ten of your men and we will make peace." At that point one of the delegation spoke up. "You know that I am the chief of our tribe. I am worth ten men. Kill me so that the score can be equaled and the fighting stopped." So they did. In the presence of all the people, the chief was put to death. And the fighting stopped. When shortly after this the missionary came and explained the meaning of Christ's death, the response was immediate

10

and lasting, as even an unbeliever like John Muir was forced to notice (*Travels in Alaska*, 197-200).

There was perhaps a great deal this tribal culture was unable to understand about the gospel. Perhaps it did not appreciate Paul's discussion of conscience, or John's discourse on Christ as the Logos of God. But the central transaction between God and sinful humanity was understood at once because of an analogy existing in its corporate memory.

In American schools our children are exposed to a very different narrative. It is the story of a high school student named Holden Caulfield who runs away to New York from his boarding school in Pennsylvania. Unlike the Indian narrative, the traditions that shape the boy are given no importance. In fact, Caulfield begins the story by noting that perhaps the reader would like to know something about his parents, "and all that David Copperfield kind of crap, but I don't feel like going into it." All we know is that he has had some kind of problem in his school and wants to escape to New York to "take it easy."

In New York Holden manages to maintain his innocence despite many challenges, and in fact takes pity on all the kids who are raised in the urban jungle. He is so struck by them that he decides he would like to be a kind of "catcher in the rye." "I keep picturing all these little kids playing some game in this big field. . . . And I'm standing on the edge of some crazy cliff. What I have to do, I have to catch everybody if they start to go over the cliff —I mean if they're running and they don't look where they're going I have to come out from somewhere and *catch* them" (J. D. Salinger, *The Catcher in the Rye*, 156).

But this turns out to be more difficult than he imagines. When he comes to his sister's school he sees dirty language written all over the walls. He tries to rub some out.

I kept wanting to kill whoever'd written it. I figured . . . some perverty bum that'd sneaked in the school late at night [had written it] . . . but this one was *scratched* on, with

11

a knife or something. It wouldn't come off. It's hopeless, anyway. If you had a million years to do it in, you couldn't rub out even *half* the "Fuck you" signs in the world. It's impossible. (181, 182)

So Holden decides to hitch a ride out West, pump gas, and save money. He will build a little cabin with all the money and live there for the rest of his life. "I'd build it right near the woods, but not right *in* them, because I'd want it to be sunny as hell all the time" (179). But even this remains a dream; his sister persuades him to stay with her in New York. As the book ends, he sits watching her go around on the merry-go-round. "I felt so damn happy all of a sudden, the way old Phoebe kept going around and around" (191).

Notice what is unique to the Salinger story. Unlike the Indian story, there seems to be no way to solve the quandary of the hero, only escape to a cabin in the woods. Moreover, the hero—who is not a chief, not even an adult, but just an ordinary kid—is a solitary individual immune to all the filth he sees around him. He seems to dwell in a region altogether outside of the story. Still he is anxious to solve the problems he sees and begins rubbing out all the dirty words. He knows deep inside that he can never succeed, but he somehow manages in the end to feel good about himself and the world.

I would like to use these stories to begin our thinking about how the gospel is heard in America. Here in narrative form are the major characteristics of two cultures: one a tribal culture with its corporate mentality, its system of honor and revenge (and thus constant battles), and its strong sense of tradition. The other is middle class American culture with its strong everyman hero, the reckless and naive attacking of problems, and the final optimism that everything will turn out alright in the end.

Unlike the Indian tribe, the middle-class subculture has existed in such a close relationship with Christianity that it sometimes is difficult to distinguish what is American from what is Christian. Our form of Christianity and our identity as a people were born simultaneously. Even for us the question raised by these stories is important: which elements in culture make it possible to understand the gospel and which make such understanding difficult?

The central irony that will emerge in this study is that in spite of the massive influence of Christianity on American middle-class culture (or is it in part because of this influence?), no primary metaphor exists that captures the central dynamic of Christianity with the same force as the chief's sacrifice. The myths that do drive us, some of them developed from Christian roots, have reached the point where they contradict basic elements of the gospel. Contrast the story of the Alaskan tribe with the do-it-yourself spirit of Holden in *The Catcher in the Rye*. In spite of all his problems, we admire Holden's willingness to tackle the filthy environment around him. Unlike literary heroes of other traditions—one thinks for example of Dostoevsky's Raskolnikov—there is no guilt or suffering attached to Holden's efforts.

Indeed, there is almost no instance in our culture in which we are aware of absolute limits which require some kind of sacrificial intervention. We may plunge in and lend a hand, we may try our best to scratch out the dirtiness, but in the end everyone must "do their own time." All of this has had an important influence on the way we think about Christianity.

What Is "American"?

Before proceeding, we must dispose of an obvious question: what do we mean by "American culture"? Notice that both our stories are about "Americans." One is the story of a so-called minority culture; the other we will call middle-class culture. Culture, as we noted in the last chapter, is a complex of learned behavior shared by members of a particular group.

American culture is unusual because in it we find more than one story being told. It has been this way from the beginning. Ours is a conversation with many different voices. One of our problems has been that stronger voices have drowned out weaker ones. As a result, the story of people like Holden Caulfield has become the primary story of the American imagination. While this narrative has sometimes been influenced by outsider stories, it has ordinarily been an accident, or even violently resisted.

For purposes of this study we will focus on what is generally known as white American middle-class culture, recognizing that this is a somewhat artificial typology. Robert Bellah justifies a similar method in his recent book *Habits of the Heart*: "We have stressed the special nature of the middle class, the fact that it is not simply a 'layer' in a system of stratification, but rather a group that seeks to embody in its own continuous progress and advancement the very meaning of the American project" (151). Critics of his study have been quick to point out that such an isolation of middle-class values is not possible: have not minority cultures made a decisive impact on this "mainstream"? More to the point, are there not regional variations, such as New England and the South, that differ in dramatic ways from other regions?

We will take these questions seriously in two ways. First we will describe that complex of values that we think of as white middle-class America. These values are ordinarily associated with suburban America, what we might call "mall culture." This description must be taken as an ideal type which may not exist in pure form but which, as an ideal, has certainly exerted great influence—not least on these minority cultures. Part of the reason for this focus is the social location of the author: a white male born and raised in the suburban Midwest. Our study will ask: what is the impact of these core values on our perception of the gospel?

But secondly we will more briefly note influences in the other direction. More and more we are beginning to note the role minority cultures are playing in our American self-consciousness. Indeed, the tensions we experience result partly from the fact that the values of minority cultures probe weaknesses in our middle-class self-image. Take as only one example the problem Americans feel of basic disconnection from their own past and therefore from needed sources of nourishment. Commentators on all sides note that we are an abstracted people. Yet black American culture possesses a deep (and sometimes painful) sense of its past, thus offering a much needed model of connectedness.

So after asking about the influence of middle-class values on our understanding of the gospel, we will acknowledge that this is not the whole story. Other American voices in our larger conversation have different perceptions of the Good News. We will ask then to what extent the distortions of the gospel in our middle-class culture are due to our cultural monologue (what anthropologists call ethnocentricity). Could it be that our failure to sustain our part in the dialogue with our neighbors across town (to say nothing of other nations) has impeded not only our witness, but our ability to hear certain voices of Scripture itself?

What Has Christianity to Do with American Culture?

Much has been written about American culture, from the Frenchman Alexis de Tocqueville to the most recent study of Robert Bellah and his colleagues, *Habits of the Heart*. Still, we in a sense know less about ourselves than about others. In some ways we might still agree with Clyde Kluckhohn when he says of American culture: "Of this culture in the anthropological sense we know less than of Eskimo culture" (229).

At the same time, in the last fifteen years we have been exposed to thinking about the relation of the gospel to many Third World cultures. This discussion of the "contextualization of the gospel" has done much to help us understand the missionary task and our limited Western understanding of the gospel. These studies provide us with categories to facilitate our discussion of how well or poorly the gospel has been contextualized into Western culture. We have assumed on the one hand that the gospel has been thoroughly assimilated by Western culture, while on the other we complain loudly about the resulting distortions of the gospel. Both assumptions need fresh examination, as we shall see.

There is of course a long tradition of Christian comment on the American project. On the one hand, certain Christians have always believed that America is somehow special in the eyes of God, a city set on the hill. We will see later that this idea, rooted in the Puritan period, has continued throughout our history. Josiah Strong, for example, argued a hundred years ago that "God with infinite wisdom and skill is training the Anglo-Saxon race for an hour sure to come. . . . This powerful race will move down upon Mexico . . . and South America, out upon the islands of the sea. . . . God . . . is . . . preparing in our civilization the die with which to stamp the nations . . . [and] he is preparing mankind to receive our impress" (*Our Country*, 174, 175, 178). Very few today would put matters in quite these terms, but this same spirit continues in contemporary public figures who argue that the Constitution was inspired by God.

On the other hand, others are quick to spot developments in America as especially expressive of human fallenness. Some of these people argue that America was perhaps once God's special place, but it recently has become captive to anti-Christian and secular values. These voices indicate that only the radical judgment of God can save us from ourselves. Evangelism is often partly seen as delivering people from the evil influences of American culture.

The late Francis Schaeffer was a moderate and sometimes eloquent exponent of this second point of view. His view of evangelism involved "taking the roof off" people.

That is, he wanted people to see that the positive values they held—love, integrity, or even a general faith in God—were often incompatible with the larger cultural and philosophical structures of which they partook. His last book, *A Christian Manifesto*, is a call back to values he believed lay beneath the founding of our country. Os Guinness has recently argued a similar position with more nuance and sensitivity. Taking America as uniquely expressive of modern values, he has argued that "the church contributed to the creation of the modern world. Soon she was committed to that world without reservation. Before long she was hopelessly contaminated—in the world and up to her neck" (*The Gravedigger File*, 25).

Both points of view would find adherents today. But however we might evaluate our culture, we must first seek to understand it. Our first work is to understand the values into which we have been socialized, and only then note their strengths and weaknesses. Though these two procedures mutually influence each other, they must be distinguished in principle. Interestingly, those most critical (or laudatory) of American culture seem to assume that their analysis is the truly objective one. The cautions we are making simply recognize that all analysis and criticism must realize the extent to which cultural values inform all we do. As Sydney Ahlstrom says of modern analyses of American life, "Even when he is radically critical of society, [the critic] often ignores both the social circumstances of his protest and the historical sources of his critique" (*Religious History*, xiii).

A more objective analysis of culture must proceed on the assumption of "cultural relativity," which we examined in the last chapter. It implies that each cultural system must be understood on its own terms, and that elements in that culture need first to be understood by their function in the cultural "logic." As Christians we can engage in such analysis because we believe all people were created in the image of God with a fundamental mandate to "fill the earth." Moreover, in spite of the fall into sin, God's common grace continues to preserve a general order. He causes the rain to fall on the just and unjust, and thus demonstrates his concern for all peoples of the earth.

Further, as Paul puts it, in sending Christ into the world, God now "commands all people everywhere to repent. For he has set a day when he will judge the world" (Acts 17:30, 31). That is, God calls people from within the particular setting—"the boundaries of their habitation" (v. 26)—which he has allotted them. In Scripture God does not love people in the abstract, but in actual situations. In the Old Testament, for example, the monarchy was accepted as a cultural form that could express the human mandate to rule. Though the people often perverted it and made it idolatrous, Deuteronomy 17:14-20 indicates that God intended to use this social structure for his purposes.

Our thinking about discipleship, then, must begin with a thorough understanding of our culture. While most social scientists admit that it is impossible for discussions of culture to be value free, they would insist that all value judgments must be made by the logic of a given culture. If it is impossible to be purely descriptive in analyzing a culture—Scripture indeed is not neutral with respect to culture—objective description is part of the work of all cultural understanding.

The tension between American culture and the gospel, however, is often intolerable. At some point we must leave off understanding and begin evaluating our culture by biblical and theological norms. In Scripture this evaluation is the clear prophetic judgment on elements in culture, and what God's people have done with those elements. Since the Fall humanity does not use culture in the way God intended. As a result, God's program for human culture must in the end be his work—the new heaven and earth which God promises will come from him down from heaven (Rev. 21:2). As Richard Mouw reminds us, we wait for the time when the "filling of the earth will be harnessed and remolded for the sake of God's glory," though we "wait" actively, seeking the city which is to come (*When the Kings Come Marching In*, 75).

Our analysis then will first seek to understand how American values function in middle-class life. Then we will ask how these values enhance or impede our understanding of the gospel—that world-changing revelation that God was in Christ reconciling all things to himself, especially as described in Scripture. Our goal is to discover more clearly how Americans are hearing the gospel, so that we may be more faithful witnesses and more consistent disciples.

Our study will proceed by evaluating three complexes of values: Americans' materialist bias, their temperamental optimism, and their individualism. These values are not necessarily unique to America, but it is clear they are distinctive of the American middle class. Following this we will inquire about the particular strengths and weaknesses of these values, a process facilitated by closer attention to minority voices. Finally, we will reflect on how this American story might help us develop a more coherent strategy of mission and Christian growth.

How Do Gospel and Culture Interact?

Every religious expression is rooted in culture. This truism of anthropology has sometimes been ignored or even denied by Christians. But our study will work with this assumption. It is well illustrated in the following analysis:

> Normally, our experience with central elements of culture—with a concept of God, for example—is highly colored by the culture passed on to us by our parents. Scholars do not take for granted that the images of God, and the complex of attitudes deemed appropriate for approaching God, are exactly the same in every culture, even of those which are generically Christian. Rather, in differ-

19

ent cultures, systems of worship and liturgy, of preaching and of practice, subtly build up quite distinctive languages of the soul. (W. Petersen, M. Novak, and P. Gleason, *Concepts of Ethnicity*, 51)

To ask how a particular culture will hear and respond to the gospel is first to ask what kind of people exist in that place. What the view of God might be in America, for example, would inevitably reflect the way Americans understand themselves and their world. Juan Luis Segundo perceptively says of North Americans: "No one feels truly free if he cannot have his own place, where he can plant tomatoes or roses as he chooses. That is his *private domain*, where he can do what he wants. . . . And it is not surprising that such a society would fashion an image of God in which he was the 'private,' independent being *par excellence*" (*Our Idea of God*, 67-68). In the Indian culture, by contrast, identity and understanding arise out of community concerns, and God therefore would relate himself to this dynamic. It goes without saying that such imbeddedness will constrict the gospel. But this is a problem of being finite and fallen—it is not in any sense a particular problem of being American (or Indian!).

But the opposite is true as well: every culture can receive the gospel. Put another way, no culture is so fallen or perverted that the Good News cannot be communicated in its terms. This is not only a matter of language—the problem of translating terms cross-culturally is familiar—but also of cultural forms. Initially the gospel must be seen as what is culturally possible. Of course, the gospel in turn will have its own impact and expand what was originally thought possible. But some common ground is prerequisite.

Communication and attendant behavioral change must take place from the known to the unknown (see Charles Kraft). The gospel is a fruit of revelation and is undiscoverable by natural means. But this does not mean that, even in the process of revelation, it fell out of heaven. It came initially

20

in language and forms that people could understand. God spoke about care for children and about the neighbor's property. At a certain point, however, both the language and the forms were found to be inadequate wineskins to hold the "new thing" God was doing. The language and forms were transformed—God wanted after all a universal family and a new creation. A similar dynamic is at work in any communication of the gospel today.

Let us think of this process of communication, and resulting spiritual growth, as taking place on four levels. The first level is the basic communion we share with others in our culture by virtue of creation in God's image and our participation in common grace. Because of the intrinsic goodness of creation—God's image in us and his sustaining activity—we share basic features of our worldview with non-Christians in our culture. This makes possible a basic level of communication that relies on and grows out of our common experience. We often speak of Christianity and culture as though these were completely different realities. But this is clearly a mistake; Christianity is inevitably expressed in terms of some culture, and culture results from human creativity within God-given structures. As Dutch theologian Herman Bavinck put this: "mankind is by general revelation preserved in its existence, maintained in its unity, and enabled to continue and to develop its history" (*Reasonable Faith,* 59).

But since we live in a fallen world we cannot rest on this first level of communication. Because we are both God's creatures and fallen, we interpret and expropriate elements of creation sometimes with nobility and goodness, and sometimes with spite and greed. Equally important, we all experience the tensions and pain that come from fallenness, and the aspirations and hopes that come from our creation in the likeness of God. Whether it is in a hospital waiting room or a university graduation line, we share hopes and pains, raising questions we all must answer: why is there pain in the

21

world? What is the meaning of the goals our society has set for us?

These questions produce tensions which demand resolution; the process of response to such experiences we might call the dialectic of growth. To be human is to reflect on our experience and seek on a second level an ever larger frame of reference for our answers. The questions and hopes our culture raises sooner or later suggest transcendent questions, what Peter Berger has called "rumors of angels." Are the pains we suffer and the hopes we know ultimately irreconcilable? Can they only be reconciled by denying the reality of either the pain (cf. Christian Science) or the hope (cf. Existentialism)?

For people in the West, and for Americans in particular, it is at the point of such "existential" questions that the claims of the gospel become relevant. But this is not the case for many other cultures. In the Philippines, for example, basic issues such as survival or physical safety are more pressing, producing tensions which demand resolution and motivate behavior and reflection. Good News for *these* people must in some way relate to such fundamental questions. It is the Christian claim that ultimately for both cultures only submission to the purposes of God revealed in Christ can provide the larger rationale to make sense of life.

At this point, of course, the gospel provides values which transcend those of our culture and move us a level further. But even here our discipleship must be carried out in the flesh and blood of our culture. Though we must find our meaning in God and his purposes, it will inevitably be expressed in the cultural forms we inherit. The assumption we make is that redemption fulfills and extends rather than repeals the purposes of creation. Christ died not to make us angels, but to make us fully human. In this discussion, he died to make us an American expression of God's purposes. This means he will radically question certain aspects of our culture and refine or affirm others. But in any case, the sphere of common grace is enlarged and enhanced after conversion. Christians not infrequently find themselves working with non-Christians to bring about justice in their culture.

The final or fourth step is what we might call prophetic discipleship. Here the growth process includes a response to new challenges (and aspirations) in light of this larger commitment and our new setting. Engineering might be seen as part of our call to care for the earth; medicine and art as images of God's redemptive work. This larger setting still includes the peculiar American situation, but now this is seen in the light of the community of God's people to which we belong and the purposes of God laid out in Scripture. These latter have become part of the "context" in which discipleship is carried out. Parts of this context will be affirmed and elaborated, parts will be challenged or reformed.

This process will occupy us at length in the conclusion. But for now it may help to lay this out in the following diagram:

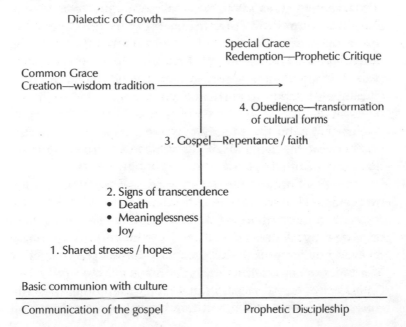

23

Christ in Culture or Christ against Culture?

It is clear already that we cannot conceive of the relation between the gospel and culture in any single way. Culture itself is changing and dynamic, and the purposes of our involvement in it are many and varied. Richard Niebuhr in his classic study *Christ and Culture* recognized in his conclusion that the relationship between Christ and culture is dependent on our faith, our historical position, and our duties. We would supplement that observation by proposing a continuum. Initial communication has to assume that in some sense Christ is in culture—God's call initially comes to people through their own experience and history (what Calvin calls the "general call"). But as soon as a person or group responds to Christ, a tension is felt between the demands of following Christ and following cultural norms. Sometimes, say in political activity, the tension may appear to place Christ and culture in paradox (see Mark Noll, *One Nation under God?*); at other times, say in the workplace, Christ can be seen as the transformer of culture. In general, though, as a person's (or group's) experience with God and his Word grows, the potential for taking elements of culture captive for the purposes of the kingdom seems to increase. So the nature of a Christian's relation to particular vocational values will depend on the history of Christian influence on that vocation. A Christian in business today may see a more positive relation between the demands of her work and those of her faith than, say, a Christian lawyer.

One's attitude toward these things is determined finally by the answer one gives to a fundamental question: Does conversion imply that one way of viewing the world, that provided by American culture, is replaced by another, provided by Scripture? This seems to be the view of Lesslie Newbigin in his excellent study *Foolishness to the Greeks: The Gospel and Western Culture*. Of the change that comes through conversion he says: "Though that other [Christian] way of understanding the world can in no way be reached by any logical step from the axioms of this [secular] one, nevertheless that other way does offer a wider rationality that embraces and does not contradict the rationality of this" (54). However, in the end that larger rationality becomes a radically different plausibility structure (cf. p. 62). Only as we engage ourselves in God's struggle in Scripture will we properly "understand" his person. At this point Scripture and tradition begin reciprocally to relate. Jacques Ellul expresses a similar view in his *Ethics of Freedom*:

> The message of God uses the cultural modes of a specific time and place and enters into them. Then there is contradiction; the difference between the content of revelation and that of the particular culture. . . . Then there is expropriation; the cultural schema or concept is absorbed by the content of revelation and the cultural sense is expropriated in favor of the revealed sense. (164)

Both Newbigin and Ellul emphasize the radical break as if now the values of culture must themselves be displaced by God's grace. The cultural sense is "expropriated in favor of the revealed sense" in Ellul's terms; it is an altogether different plausibility structure, in Newbigin's phrase. But this laudable attempt to preserve the radical character of Christ's work risks undermining the value that God placed in his created order, and that Christ's death and resurrection extends. As a result, any motivation for exploring and developing cultural and creational forms for their own sake is weakened.

Our approach is to assume that God is already at work in culture both to preserve and enhance his creative purposes. All of this must be understood finally in terms of the gospel, but this understanding does not confer value so much as put it in its proper context. We have then an ambiguous attitude toward culture—it can facilitate communication and understanding, or it can impede it. Yet this ambivalence does

25

not obscure our fundamental faith in the goodness and integrity of the created order. Since the Fall the forces of evil
have distorted this order, but they have not been able to
overthrow it. Two examples may be helpful before turning to
the larger discussion.

A major issue for many people today is the environment. Less pressing than during the oil crisis ten years ago,
this still is a major social and political issue. When a Christian
becomes concerned with preserving the environment—perhaps choosing public transport rather than driving a car to
work—he or she will often share many values with others. It
is clear to many Christians and non-Christians that our own
survival is tied to the quality of our environment. Here is a
real public concern, as opposed to an artificially constructed
one.

But what happens, for example, when water needs for
urban areas conflict with preservation of our wilderness
areas? In the debate about which should take precedence,
more ultimate questions become inescapable. Can human
identity in any sense be understood in any sense separately
from nature? Are the two simply one organism (cf. the Gaia
hypothesis)? This becomes very soon a religious rather than
simply a philosophical question, because it implies allegiance
and faith commitment. Here, we would argue, the gospel
offers the only finally satisfying framework for addressing
this issue. Cultural forms may dictate the terms of the discussion, but religious commitments will finally evaluate these
terms.

One final example is the discussion of family problems
and child rearing. We will note from time to time how culturally determined these issues are: by the age of six months
the socialization process is well along. As Christians we will
inevitably share a broad range of tensions produced by our
culture: independent development versus commitment in
marriage, or the need for encouraging initiative in our
teenagers versus the need for control and value develop-

ment. No one living in our society can really avoid these pressures, and here we can share a large area of conversation with our non-Christian neighbors. But what do we do when the tensions become too intense? The independent child (or spouse!) can no longer tolerate a situation that to her has become oppressive. Again, even the terms of the problem are cultural. But the response to these tensions inevitably is colored by religious or faith commitments, and here the gospel becomes relevant. What is the nature of authority in the family? Is the covenant of marriage meant to reflect some larger (transcendent) communion? Or is it merely meant to serve the needs of the individuals involved? These are the questions we all wrestle with as Americans and as Christians. And it is in these parameters that we must both communicate and live out the demands of the gospel.

Let us return to the stories with which we opened this chapter. One reflected the traditional and communal nature of human life, the other the pain of individual ambition in a blighted world. Each of these will allow part of the gospel to be seen, but may make other parts hard to see. This fact alone shows us how important it is that we listen to each other's stories (and testimonies), those close by and those further away. We who have been shaped by the American middle-class values must begin our Christian pilgrimage at home.

Allan D'Archangelo, *FULL MOON*, 1962
(from the collection of Sydney and Frances Lewis;
used by permission of the Virginia Museum of Fine Arts)

CHAPTER THREE

The Virgin Land

Wilderness is a temporary condition through which we are passing to the promised land.

—Cotton Mather

WHAT ARE THE ROOTS OF THE VALUES THAT SHAPE AMERI-cans? What influence have these had on our comprehension of the gospel? We cannot review the whole story (or all of the stories) here, but we must make some historical soundings to discover where we have come from. We will probe in three directions. In the first section we will examine the impact of our natural (later the artificial) environment on us, focusing on the habits and practices this has encouraged; in the second we will consider our incurable optimism under the rubric the American Dream; finally, we will consider American indi-vidualism as symbolized by the American Adam. We admit that such generalizations greatly oversimplify a complex situa-tion. Moreover, much of what we say applies to other cultures as well. We are after, however, what is distinctive, not what is unique, to the American middle class. In a general sense, we will argue that Americans are philosophically pragmatist, temperamentally optimistic, and psychologically humanist. Any genuine understanding of Christianity in this setting inevitably bears the marks of these values, for good or ill.

From Wilderness to City: The Pilgrim's Progress

In 1893 the historian Frederick Jackson Turner addressed the American Historical Society on "The Significance of the Frontier in American History." There he argued that

> The peculiarity of American institutions is, the fact that they have been compelled to adapt themselves to the changes of an expanding people—to the changes involved in crossing a continent, in winning a wilderness, and in developing at each area of this progress out of the primitive economic and political conditions of the frontier into the complexity of city life. (Turner, *The Frontier in American History*, 2)

Such unicausal explanations of American institutions are not popular today. Sydney Ahlstrom, for example, reminds us that equally striking as the impact of the frontier is the "persistence with which the thought, institutions, and practice of Europe and the settled East crossed the mountains and penetrated the life of the newly settled areas" (*Religious History*, 453). Still, Turner's thesis has been very influential, not the least because he says what everyone living (or visiting!) America has thought at one time or another. St. John de Crèvecoeur, the French cartographer who settled near the Hudson in the 1780s, is an example. He exclaimed:

> Many ages will not see the shores of our great lakes replenished with inland nations, nor the unknown bounds of North America entirely peopled. Who can tell how far it extends? Who can tell the millions of men whom it will feed and contain? For no European foot has as yet travelled

half the extent of this mighty continent! (In Henry Nash Smith, *Virgin Land*, 126)

From the very beginning it has been the immensity and challenge of the land, and later what was made of it, that has provided a major impetus to action and thought. Why is owning our own place so important? Whence the incredible mobility and fluidity of our people? Why must we always make ideas practical? Clearly all this has something to do with the scope and scale of the task our natural setting has put before us. As church historian Sydney Mead put it, this new person which we call the American is the result of a new land and a new space (*The Lively Experiment*, 1).

Attitudes toward the environment have been reflected in changing perceptions of the wilderness and the city. Though as a people we have become citified, our freeways are still clogged every afternoon with commuters willing to spend thirty to sixty minutes reaching their bit of the country. How the wilderness has changed from the cursed abode of the spirits for our European ancestors (and the Bible!) to something close to "the promised land" in present American thinking; conversely, how the city has changed from the center of civilized life, hearth, and home to the center of crime, unemployment, and industrial pollution—these stories are central to the account of how we middle-class Americans perceive ourselves, and to the ways we recount the gospel.

The Puritans: A Home in the Wilderness

Stephen Vincent Benét once described our Puritan fathers in these words:

They were all alone as few we know are alone.
They made a small bustling noise in an empty land.

The land immediately became not merely the setting for the

human drama, but one of the protagonists in it. It may have seemed dark, brooding, and cold, but it could not be ignored. Governor William Bradford described what the settlers in the Plymouth plantation found:

> They had now no friends to wellcome them, no inns to entertaine or refresh their weatherbeaten bodys, no houses or much less townes to repaire too. . . . And for ye season it was winter, and they that know ye winters of ye cuntrie know them to be sharp & violent, & subjects to cruell & feirce stormes. . . . Besids, what could they see but a hidious & desolate wildernes, full of wild beasts & willd men? and what multituds ther might be of them they knew not. Nether could they, as it were, goe up to ye tope of Pisgah, to vew from this wildernes a more godly cuntrie. . . . For sumer being done, all things stand upon them with a wetherbeaten face; and ye whole cuntrie, full of woods & thickets, represented a wild & savage heiw. (In Ahlstrom, 136)

The settlers' assessment of wilderness would have differed very little from that of their countrymen who remained in Europe. The sense of human isolation and the desolation these settlers faced during those first dark winters made them hanker for the civilization they had left. Their very survival depended on their ability to tame the wilds.

But unique to this project, and what set the settlers apart from their European counterparts was the sense of mission associated with their movement. God had sent them to this place. "His Divine Providence," Cotton Mather wrote in the *Magnalia Christi Americana* (1702), "hath irradiated an Indian wilderness" (1). This sense of providence was soon given a spatial dimension as the land continued to draw them. As the population increased, settlements pressed westward. More than one colonist worried about what this expansion would do to the customs of the people. Edmund Burke, from the point of view of a settled insular England, wondered what would stop them.

Already they have topped the Appalachian Mountains. From thence they behold before them an immense plain, one vast, rich, level meadow; a square of five hundred miles. Over this they would wander without a possibility of restraint; they would change their manners with their habits of life; would soon forget a government by which they were disowned; would become hordes of English Tartars; and, pouring down upon your unfortified frontiers a fierce and irresistible cavalry, become masters of your governors and your counselors. (In Turner, 33-34)

But the English leaders were not the only ones who wanted to limit settlement; even Thomas Jefferson wanted to keep settlers out of the Louisiana Purchase until "we shall be full on this side [of the Mississippi]" (in ibid.: 34). Though Manifest Destiny was not coined until a century later, there was already an inexorability to the westward movement; the land beckoned, and, as once people yearned for freedom of worship, they now yearned for freedom of movement and the economic vistas it offered.

The beginning of the 19th century represents a complex amalgam of what Perry Miller calls the intellect of the revival, confidence in a rational natural law (coming from the Enlightenment), and a down-to-earth sense of the practical. The first two of these factors we consider in more detail below. Here we wish to point out how large a role America's frontier situation played in all this. As it formed, the utilitarian character, though it had a complex root system, took its impetus from attitudes that were first expressed toward the land. When Thomas Jefferson sent Lewis and Clark on their famous expedition, it was a drama of great significance for the future. Its importance, then as now in our remembrance of it, lay on the level of imagination: this was the land that would one day become America.

During this period it was commonly argued that truly virtuous work was that done on the land with one's hands. A nameless legislator from Virginia gives a good sense of attitudes around 1830 in this speech:

But, sir, it is not the increase of population in the West which [you] ought to fear. It is the energy which the mountain breeze and western habits impart to those emigrants. They are regenerated, politically I mean, sir. They soon become *working politicians*; and the difference, sir, between a *talking* and a *working* politician is immense. The Old Dominion has long been celebrated for producing great orators; the ablest metaphysicians in policy; men that can split hairs in all abstruse questions of political economy. But at home, or when they return from Congress, they have negroes to fan them asleep. But a Pennsylvania, a New York, an Ohio, or a western Virginia statesman, though far inferior in logic, metaphysics, and rhetoric to an old Virginia statesman, has this advantage, that when he returns home he takes off his coat and takes hold of the plow. This gives him bone and muscle, sir, and preserves his republican principles pure and uncontaminated. (In Turner, 31)

Notice the assumed relation between honest work on the land and integrity, even adherence to republican principles. This complex of attitudes—called by Charles E. Eisinger the "freehold concept"—became very influential in the early part of the 19th century, and has grounded American values in rural sunshine and hard work ever since. It includes the idea that the land is the source of wealth, and everyone has a natural right to land. Work on the land confers valid title to it, and ownership of land makes a person independent, conferring social status (see Henry Nash Smith, 126).

But even more striking is the innocence of the land and its owners. It was as if work in the fresh air was itself a kind of religious activity that could purge sin (which now more and more was identified with the city). The virgin land conferred purity as well as dignity on its conquerors. Listen, for example, to James B. Lanman writing this paean to the "yeoman" during the 1830s:

34

If, as has been remarked by a distinguished statesman, cities are the sores of the political body, where the bad matter of the state is concentrated, what healthful habitudes of mind and body are afforded by agricultural enterprise! The exhilarating atmosphere of a rural life, the invigorating exercise afforded by its various occupations, the pure water, the abundance of all the necessities of subsistence, leading to early and virtuous marriages, all point to this pursuit as best adapted to the comfort of the individual man. Its beneficial bearing upon the state is no less obvious. (In Henry Nash Smith, 142)

It is possible that this picture of the land and its people was a product of jaded city dwellers discouraged by the filth and darkness of industrialization (Lanman himself was a Connecticut Yankee who lived in Michigan for only two years). Roderick Nash argues that appreciation of the wilderness began in the city (*Wilderness and the American Mind,* 44). Whatever the reality, the pristine wilderness beyond the settlements had captured the imagination of America. It had become the garden of the world where the New Adam could realize his inherent dignity.

The idea that land was a primary source of meaning and value lay behind the rhetoric used against the slave states and in support of the Homestead Act of 1862. Homesteading became the dominant image for the conquest of the West, capturing all that we are proud of in relation to the land: work gives proper title, dignity, and social status. Never mind that the Act was by all accounts a failure. By 1890 only two out of ten million had settled the West under this program, and by 1900, 35 percent of all farmers had become tenants, and the figure was rising. Concludes Henry Nash Smith: "The Homestead Act failed because it was incongruous with the industrial revolution" (184-91). This reality was all too evident in the growing cities, where during the gilded age struggle and violence were common. Now the incessant movement ceased to relate to geography—economic growth had come to replace westward movement as the frontier of civilization.

A unique aspect of the story of Christianity in America is that it has flourished in both rural and urban contexts. Indeed, George Marsden points out that fundamentalism as a movement started in the city, but survived by forming a subculture that would protect it against the monstrous urban problems (the more recent flight to the suburbs may manifest a similar fear). Exactly correct belief, Marsden argues, provided an alternative worldview to the dominant social ethos (*Fundamentalism*, 202-5). But the imagery that has flourished, especially in conservative churches, has pictured the virtue of faith in rural hues that contrast sharply with the dark wickedness resident in the city. Sandra Sizer in her study of 19th-century revival hymnody points out the contrasting images of good and evil in these hymns (*Gospel Hymns and Social Religion*, 126):

Negative	Positive
City, money making	Country, home, family
Fear, wailing, sorrow	Love, sympathy, peace

To this day the wilderness survives largely in our imagination. Just as once our Puritan ancestors dreamed of inns and settled towns to rescue them from the ravages of an untamed wilderness, so we dream of pristine wilderness areas as a retreat from urban problems. But the case could be made that the challenge once offered by the wilderness is now offered by our urban centers. Possibly the teleology that sent Americans out to reclaim the wilderness might best be focused on reclaiming our urban centers. Interestingly, Murray Melbin has recently argued that the values of people on our city streets after dark are surprisingly similar to those of our pioneer ancestors (see *Night as Frontier: Colonizing the World after Dark*).

Many people assume that urbanization and secularization have gone hand in hand. But it is increasingly clear that this new urban frontier is neither more nor less congenial to faith than was the previous one. As Mary Douglas has pointed out, traditional theories of secularization have failed grandly to account for recent revivals in religion, espcially in areas influenced by modernization and urbanization. All structures of social relations, she notes, give rise to ultimate explanations. The modern experience of bureaucracy has replaced the earlier experience with nature; neither has inhibited religion. Culture is not autonomous; it merely provides containers "in which social interests are defined and classified" (*Religion and America,* 26-36). At the very least this ought to give Christians a sense of hope and mission toward the end of our century. Before we elaborate this further we will examine our attitudes toward our physical environment and our resulting pragmatic temperament.

Early to Bed and Early to Rise

As pioneers pushed westward in their Conestoga wagons, a parallel development in the settled regions was that the habits and institutions that formed suited the need to move and build. Before the institutions came the habits. These developed under influences that were part religious—the belief in a providential planting of people in America—and part philosophical.

An important factor here was certainly the thought of John Locke. In his *Second Treatise on Civil Government* (1690) he argued that in the state of nature all men produce what is most needed. Property arises when one appropriates something from the common store for a particular use. "The labor that was mine, removing them out of that common state they were in, has fixed my property in them" (V: 28). This use of resources is "natural," and exists prior to any organized society. The latter then exists to preserve the rights to property that belong inherently to everyone. This has of course become common knowledge. Our view of rights due us follows from the view that "Government exists," as Allan Bloom points out, "to protect the product of men's labor, their property, and therewith life and liberty" (*The Closing of the American Mind*, 165).

John Locke was a Christian and probably did not intend his ideas to have the consequences they had. But note carefully that the way is prepared to understand our relation to our environment primarily in economic terms. Moreover, our right to property is principally prior to our membership in society. The temptation follows, we will see, to actually define the person in material terms, overlooking entirely the social basis both of our knowing and of our relation to creation. While property is not explicitly listed as a right in our Declaration of Independence, Thomas Paine includes it prominently in his "Rights of Man."

The one who might well symbolize our mechanical and utilitarian relation to the environment is Benjamin Franklin. His pamphlets on western settlements reveal his complete understanding of what the land meant for the future of America among the community of nations: it would forever beckon settlers, drawing off excess (and unemployed!) workers from the cities; it would create an agrarian-based society that soon would be an economic power to be reckoned with (see Henry Nash Smith, 6-8).

In Franklin's autobiography, which he intended to be an American version of John Bunyan's *Pilgrim's Progress*, Franklin enunciated the habits he felt necessary to wealth and success. All his activities were to be designed to assure maximum efficiency in controlling his environment. As his attempts to project the numbers and location of western settlers may be considered first steps toward statistical studies of population trends, so his program of character formation may presage the equally important time management schemas of our own century—indeed, one of the most prominent of these, the Franklin Institute, is based explicitly on his program.

With a young family, a debt for his printing business, and the competition of two printers "who were establish'd in the Place before me," Franklin had no time for "Taverns, Games, or Frolicks of any kind." So, he tells us in his autobiography, "I from thence consider'd Industry as a Means of obtaining Wealth and Distinction" (*Autobiography*, 143-44). It was about this time, he tells us, that he conceived the project of arriving at moral perfection. In a notebook he listed thirteen virtues.

> I determined to give a Week's strict Attention to each of the Virtues successively. Thus in the first Week my great Guard was to avoid every the least Offence against Temperance.... Like him who having a Garden to weed, does not attempt to eradicate all the bad Herbs at once, which would exceed his Reach and his Strength, but works on one of the Beds at a time, . . . so I should have, (I hoped) the encouraging Pleasure of seeing on my Pages the Progress I made in Virtue. . . . I was surpriz'd to find myself so much fuller of Faults than I had imagined, but I had the Satisfaction of seeing them diminish. . . . And it may be well my Posterity should be informed, that to this little Artifice, with the Blessing of God, their Ancestor ow'd the constant Felicity of his Life down to his 79th Year in which this is written. (151-52, 155, 157)

There are certainly Puritan roots to this program of Franklin. But his homespun philosophy ("Early to bed and early to rise, makes a man healthy, wealthy, and wise"; "A penny saved is a penny earned") was well suited to a large teeming continent in which there was so much to do and so little time. It clearly reflects as well the confident sense that the world belonged to the settler by a kind of divine right. What Franklin called principles were actually a kind of practice that has come to dominate the middle-class consciousness, and lies at the basis of the whole process we call modernization.

Impetus for this process came from the vast changes brought about by the Second Great Awakening. While this will be discussed in more detail below, here we note that an important by-product of these revivals was the practical kind of Christianity they featured. In the light of the growing social problems, according to Timothy Smith, a major impulse of Christianity in this period was utilitarian: "the hunger for an experience which would make Christianity work" (*Revivalism and Social Reform*, 145). Interestingly, he notes that though the revivals began on the frontier, their major impact by mid-century was in eastern urban areas. The waves of immigrants and industrialization were creating a new frontier of opportunity.

One who was typical of the revival mentality was Charles Finney. This evangelist, whose personal style at times recalls that of Franklin, was a major figure in the shift of consciousness that made modernization possible. Finney claimed that the desires for rest, leisure, food, and clothing were to be indulged only to the degree they aided the utility of the individual. When a housewife was contemplating the purchase of coffee, the evangelist urged: "My sister, how many Bibles and tracts have you used in this way? How many Bibles at five shillings each, might be sent by you to the heathen every year, were you willing to exercise a little self-denial?" (Moorhead, "Charles Finney," 102).

Though such scruples may seem strange even to Christians today, James Moorhead has argued that Finney "represented a general cultural transformation in the late eighteenth and early nineteenth centuries whereby time-thrift, utility, and methodical work habits became cardinal virtues. . . . [He] was enunciating values by which a number of his co-religionists were creating a modern economic regime based upon impersonal rules of efficiency and productivity" (103-4).

The hold of the natural world on our imagination is perhaps best seen perhaps in the writings of our prophet of hope Ralph Waldo Emerson. So engrossed was he with the natural that he even felt that tidy and civilized Unitarianism was an obstruction to faith. People, he felt, had become captive to the commercial and cultural interests of Boston. Though he is identified with the romantic movement, clearly Emerson was responding to an American situation. His was a religious demonstration, Perry Miller argues, against the rationalism of his fathers (*Transcendentalists*, 5-6). But in another sense he was giving voice to Americans' fundamental attachment to the natural.

In his famous essay on "Nature," Emerson rhapsodizes: "Give me health and a day, and I will make the pomp of emperors ridiculous. The dawn is my Assyria . . . broad noon shall be my England" (*Essays*, 43). We have no need of these traditions; we may find in our own world all that is true and beautiful. "The invariable mark of wisdom is to see the miraculous in the common. . . . Man and woman and their social life, poverty, labor, sleep, fear, fortune, are known to you. Learn that none of these things is superficial, but that each phenomenon has its roots in the faculties and affections of the mind. Whilst the abstract question occupies your intellect, nature brings it in the concrete to be solved by your hands" (80). Again, the keynote is the discovery not only of self but of goodness. Truth will come in our work, with our hands, and in our plot of ground: "Though the wide universe is full of good, no kernel of nourishing corn can come to him but through his toil bestowed on that plot of ground which is given to him to till" (176).

In March 1845, Henry David Thoreau set out on what was to become a parable of American ideals. He borrowed an axe and built himself a wooden hut on Walden Pond, near Concord, Massachusetts, where he lived for two years. He testified: "I went to the woods because I wished to live deliberately, to front only the essential facts of life, and see if I could not learn what it had to teach, and not, when I came to die, discover that I had not lived. . . . I wanted to live deep and suck all the marrow out of life" (*Walden*, 66). To know life

41

by experience, firsthand, was clearly for him a religious quest. For Christianity, he notes, has concluded "somewhat hastily" that our chief end is to glorify God, but Thoreau wished to learn for himself what his chief end might be in his experience with nature.

In all of this, Americans learned to define themselves by their relation to their work—their interaction with their environment. This history has had curiously ambiguous results. It has produced people with an incredible vitality and creativity. But it has sometimes made it difficult for these people to define themselves in genuinely human terms. Thoreau may be required reading by both the street person of Berkeley and the backpacking lawyer in San Francisco, but it has not helped them understand each other. Ironically, Emerson admitted once that he did not belong to the poor, nor the poor to him; the Homestead Act made no provision for the Negro (or the Indian!) in the West. These facts suggest a certain unreality to our experience with nature. John Updike, in an essay on Emerson, concluded that while Emerson did not create our expansionist exploitive verve, he did give it a high-minded apology. "Can it be true that, along with our sweet independence and informality, there is something desolate and phantasmal, a certain thinness of experience, that goes with our thinness of civilization?" ("Review," 123-25).

An inherent tension is evident in the pioneer story that Americans to this day have been unable to resolve. It was seen in the heroes of this time. Was Daniel Boone the pioneer of civilization, or the child of the wilderness? Was Thoreau a rebel against the artificialities of civilization or merely a pioneer of a higher human order? We have always been uneasy about the city even when we cannot live without its luxuries. Civilization seems to place an artificial screen over what is natural and innocent, even as it provides most of us a comfortable paycheck. It seems we appreciate both city and wilderness when they allow us freedom and independence, whether economic or social. Indeed, the ideal experience with nature today is widely believed to be the solitude provided by the wilderness areas. But notice that whatever Americans do in the country or the city seems to further their psychic isolation, one of the costs of the love of freedom. This tension is best seen today in the love affair with the omnipresent recreational vehicle. With these one can head for the wilds every weekend; be alone, but take along all the comforts of home.

A University of the Marketplace: Pragmatism

While Emerson may have been one of the first to encourage Americans to find culture and beauty in their backyard, plenty of them were anxious to make a virtue of this necessity. In the 1850s the so-called land grant, or agricultural and mechanical colleges began. These were conceived on the principle that the Latin and moral philosophy taught in the rapidly multiplying colleges had little use in real life. As some wag quipped: "What good is it to say 'hello' in five languages if you don't have enough to eat?" What people need to know is methods of fertilizing, crop rotation, and selective breeding (Furnas, *Social History*, 746).

In keeping with this American tendency, graduates of these schools were able to work out their own salvation, discovering their identity in working the land. Meanwhile, their professors, or at least the philosophers among them, were plowing the down-to-earth furrow of utilitarianism developed by John Stuart Mill in England. Charles Peirce, born in 1839 in Cambridge, Massachusetts, was an example. Though he never wrote a book, his papers exerted a major influence that continues to this day, and is especially evident in that movement of philosophy called Pragmatism.

The major thrust of Peirce's work was that all statements, if they are to be meaningful, ought to be translated into hypothetical "if-then" propositions. Our knowledge needs to be shown true or false by being "operationalized." In an article

43

that first appeared in the *Popular Science Monthly* (!) in 1878, he argued that our idea of anything is our idea of its sensible effects. Clarity is tested by its practical effects. He wrote: "The essence of belief is the establishment of a habit, and different beliefs are distinguished by the different modes of action to which they give rise" (*Essential Writings*, 144). So the validity of beliefs is found in their effects, though Peirce claimed he was not making any assertion about the nature of truth. He says, "Metaphysics is a subject much more curious than useful, the knowledge of which, like that of a sunken reef, serves chiefly to enable us to keep clear of it" (156-57).

Peirce's famous follower William James took these ideas further (some think beyond what Peirce intended) in his famous lectures on Pragmatism given in 1907. For James not only the meaning of statements, but also their truth is decided by the effects they produce. "What difference would it practically make to anyone," he wants to know, "if this notion rather than that notion were true? If no practical difference whatever can be traced, then the alternatives mean practically the same thing, and all dispute is idle" (*Pragmatism*, 42). Grounding thinking in our practice leads to the suggestion (first made by Peirce) that beliefs are really rules for action; theories are instruments rather than enigmas. In general, this means looking toward "cash-value" consequences, rather than away from life toward some abstract realm of principles. Pragmatism asks:

> "Grant an idea or belief to be true, . . . what concrete difference will its being true make in anyone's actual life?" . . . *True ideas are those that we can assimilate, validate, corroborate and verify. False ideas are those that we cannot.* That is the practical difference it makes to us to have true ideas. . . . The practical value of true ideas is thus primarily derived from the practical importance of their objects to us. (97-98)

One could not find a better illustration of this than in the person of Christopher Newman, hero of the novel *The*

American, written by James's brother Henry some twenty years before the famous 1907 lectures. Newman is a rich American on tour in Europe, pitting his homespun dignity against the titled, storied nobility of Paris. He encounters an American clergyman by the name of Babcock, who adores Goethe and tries to embue Newman with some of his own spiritual starch, but Newman's "personal texture was too loose to admit of stiffening."

> His mind could no more hold principles than a sieve can hold water. He admired principles extremely, and thought Babcock a mighty fine little fellow for having so many. He accepted all that his high-strung companion offered him, and put them away in what he supposed to be a very safe place; but poor Babcock never afterwards recognized his gifts among the articles that Newman had in daily use. (*The American*, 83)

Only those things that can be brought into everyday use are of real value, though Newman could spare, as most Americans can, real admiration for people with spiritual principles.

This pragmatism does not reflect a native incapacity for abstract thinking so much as the presence of more pressing concerns. John Dewey took a further step to insist that philosophy does not begin in wonder, as the Greeks have said, but with a problem. Philosophy is less like an intellectual quandary than a river to cross. Thinking, then, is sorting alternative courses of action. Dewey's fundamental contribution not only to philosophy but to educational practice was to insist on the interrelation between knowing and doing, and the role of experience in learning. He argued:

> Reason is experimental intelligence, conceived after the pattern of science, and used in the creation of social arts; it has something to do. It liberates man from the bondage of the past, due to ignorance and accident hardened into custom. It projects a better future and assists man in its

realization. And its operation is always subject to test in experience. The plans which are formed, the principles which man projects as guides of reconstructive action, are not dogmas. They are hypotheses to be worked out in practice, and to be rejected, corrected and expanded as they fail or succeed in giving our present experience the guidance it requires. (*Reconstruction in Philosophy*, 96)

This preference for making our environment into an instrument for our own progress, ironically portrayed in Allan D'Archangelo's painting at the beginning of this chapter, has had great impact on our corporate life. It has encouraged, for example, our tendency to define our problems in quantifiable terms. Statistics often play the role of final arbiter in any question—especially those resulting from opinion polls dissected for us in the morning newspaper. If something can be counted, it must be real.

Of course this has given America an edge in the development of technical solutions, but alternately, nothing is solved but that which can be put into quantifiable terms. Our incessant effort to bring our environment under control has given us a "national sweet tooth" for modelling and packaged solutions. Case studies and models ostensibly provide "paradigms" for approaches to problem solving in which the parts apparently are interchangeable.

The point of focus for these discussions is our educational system. The March 1983 issue of the *Music Educators Journal*, for example, carried a long discussion on the value of music in our schools. On the one side were the utilitarians who argued that the arts are one of the few remaining places where our feelings of national pride can be built up, and that any discipline that believes in its own lack of utility is doomed. On the other side were those who argued that it was precisely this resistance to assimilating the arts to "instrumental values" that made music vital to humanistic education.

The problem for educators, of course, is how to measure

noninstrumental values. Today the feeling is widespread that our colleges and universities do not adequately teach students to think for themselves. Though they are often adequately trained in the technical fields necessary for career placement, students lack a larger sense of direction. "The crisis of our time relates," Ernest L. Boyer noted in an address to the American Council on Education in October 1986, "not to the technical capacity of students but to their inability to place technical skills in larger contexts" (untitled manuscript of the address). It is not surprising that colleges today are reasonably successful in teaching competence. But, asks Boyer who is head of the Carnegie foundation for the advancement of teaching, competence to what end? Here the Carnegie study found a virtual paralysis in higher education. Almost without exception neither administrators nor students could articulate, let alone defend, the objectives of their university.

The result is that university students are exposed to everything, but nothing is allowed to claim ultimate value. It is all instrumental; the meaning provided by overarching values has been lost. So Allan Bloom concludes his recent discussion of these things:

> Indiscriminateness is a moral imperative because its opposite is discrimination. This folly means that men are not permitted to seek for the natural human good and admire it when found, for such discovery is coeval with the discovery of the bad and contempt for it. Instinct and intellect must be suppressed by education. The natural soul is to be replaced with an artificial one. (*The Closing of the American Mind*, 30)

It would be unwise to undervalue the strength of the American educational system. Competence and technical skills do prepare students to compete successfully in the job market of our industrialized society. Moreover, within academia itself is a growing awareness that the weaknesses of the Western intellectual tradition in its American form relate to an inability to integrate theory and practice. Many of the recent critiques of this tradition (by, for example, Charles Taylor and Alasdair MacIntyre) have come to focus on communal practice as the context in which theory develops. Robert Bellah has pointed out that the way is open to recover the importance of religious commitment as a reflection on and integrator of practice.

In our discussion of education, this implies that evaluating competence and skill acquisition is important, but that these should reflect a larger value framework. Ernest Boyer concluded the speech we have quoted by saying: "The focus of the evaluation we pursue should be on integration, not fragmentation, on creativity, not simply recall, on larger perspectives, not on isolated facts."

In Search of a "Practical" Gospel

What can we conclude about the significance of this for our understanding of the gospel? What container has our national experience provided for us?

On the one hand, all of this focuses on the material affluence of our way of life. David Potter has argued that abundance has tied together our rural and urban contexts and influenced decisively our American character (*People of Plenty*, 147). We have had the luxury of both the space and the resources to pursue equal opportunity. Once it was the fertility of the land that beckoned, now it is the splendor of the weekend sale in the mall. The town center (or the mall), argue Paul and Percival Goodman, "is the container of the work, the public pleasures, and the market. . . . (The city) is a department store. Everywhere, in every corridor, as at a permanent fair, are on display the products that make it worthwhile to get up in the morning to go to work, and to work efficiently in order to have at the same time the most money and the most leisure" (*Communitas*, 138).

But our great strength, our material success, is on the other hand also a potential weakness. For as C. Vann Woodward points out, like the South before the Civil War, we have allowed our whole way of life to be identified with one institution—the economy. "Some of us have also tended to identify the security of the country with the security of that institution" (*The Burden of Southern History*, 184).

Indeed, we are overwhelmed by that institution. For we may enjoy our first, or periodic, visit to the shopping mall, our contemporary equivalent to Goodman's town center. But sooner or later we begin to lose track of ourselves. Our senses are numbed by the extravagant displays of our department stores. When traveling, one sees the same stores, similar malls, and we lose our sense of place, of being rooted.

> take it from me kiddo
> believe me
> my country, 'tis of
>
> you, land of the Cluett
> Shirt Boston Garter and Spearmint
> Girl With The Wrigley Eyes (of you
> land of the Arrow Ide
> and Earl &
> Wilson
> Collars) of you i
> sing: land of Abraham Lincoln and Lydia E. Pinkham
> land above all of Just Add Hot Water and Serve—
> from every B.V.D.
>
> let freedom ring
>
> amen.   e. e. cummings

One of the great ironies of American culture is that, though shaped in such large measure by its physical environment, it encourages us to put down no roots in that environment. It seems our efficiency has been bought at some cost, and this exchange has put an indelible mark on our under-standing and our communication of the gospel.

From this discussion we can point to a preoccupation with acting out and operationalizing our faith. Though as a result we can be very efficient, at the same time we face a constant temptation to confuse questions of truth with those of power. If what works is what is true, then, contrary to what William James intended, power—and its material counter-part wealth—tend to be self-justifying in America. We as-sume work is necessary and will produce value. Calculated work determines most of our thinking process; when Thomas Watson encouraged his employees to "think," he really meant work carefully and plan ahead.

Let us review the components of this pragmatic materi-alism and then reflect on the significance of this for commu-nicating the gospel.

a. On the Move

From the beginning Americans have been people on the move. The land was big and beckoning. Because there was usually plenty of space, privacy and identity have often been expressed in spatial terms. Edward Hall explored this in his book *The Hidden Dimension*. In Europe it is common to join a stranger at a restaurant table and not expect to talk; in America physical proximity, at least for suburbanites, means some social interaction is necessary. This is because privacy is usually considered in spatial terms: children need their own room when they reach a certain age, and the family dream is a private home with a yard. In general identity is associated with having and defending one's own "turf."

That Americans have always been a people on the move is evident even from the layout of the traditional downtown. While cities in Europe (and Latin America) are organized around a central square or plaza, American cities stretch along a straight main street. There is really no center; everywhere is on the way to somewhere else. Today the major organizing principle of our metropolitan areas is the freeway, that monument to American mobility. Whereas in Europe cathedrals often occupy the central square, in America churches now vie with each other (and with giant shopping centers) to locate themselves near the major freeway. Landscape is something we pass through, now usually on superhighways, on the way to somewhere else. Movement has become an end in itself; space has become a commodity to be used up.

Freedom, like privacy, is often thought of in spatial terms. To be free is to be unencumbered, able to move without hindrance. When problems arise, freedom means that one can move on, to a new city, a new job, and, all too often, a new marriage. Accordingly, we have taken to use the language of travel to speak of our moral pilgrimage: "I use to feel that pre-marital sex was wrong, but I have moved beyond that." I can still hear the voice of Hank Snow, the country singer of a generation ago: "I'm movin' on / I'll soon be gone / It's all over now 'cause you've broken your vow / so I'm movin' on." From the Conestoga to the RV, we hanker to move on to greener pastures.

Because going is as important as arriving, the temptation is always present to confuse movement with progress. Like the state and park stickers on the sides of a Winnebago, what we have seen becomes a measure of how "far we have come," and how good life has been. Movement has become merely linear. As Allan Bloom put it:

> *Movement* takes the place of progress, which has a definite direction, a good direction, and is a force that controls men. Progress was what the old revolutions were evidence of. Movement has none of this naive, moralistic nonsense in it. Motion rather than fixity is our condition—but motion without any content or goal not imposed on it by man's will. (221-22)

b. In a Hurry

Because there is so much ground to cover, Americans have always been a people in a hurry. Our language reflects the importance of hurrying: we are rushed, under the gun, under pressure, hassled, facing a deadline, or pressed for time. One of the great ironies for anyone who has spent time in the Third World is that though we are a people known for our labor-saving devices, no one ever seems to have any extra time. In fact, there is an inverse correlation between possession of paraphernalia for leisure—summer homes, outside patios, boats, etc.—and time to enjoy these things. Those most likely to afford such amenities are least likely to have time to enjoy them! From morning till night one rushes through life. Meanwhile, minorities among us seem to have ample time to while away long summer evenings on front porches or street curbs.

Speed is an important American value because it saves time and conquers space. So the leisurely (and exquisite) Highway One down the coast of California has hardly a car, while Interstate Five, that drab line through California's central valley, is often bumper to bumper.

These attitudes toward space and time reflect our increasingly urbanized environment. Many commentators have pointed out that even our taste in spectator sports has changed to reflect this trend. Roger Angell argued that our growing infatuation with football instead of baseball has to do with our inclination to prefer speed and power rather than wisdom and concentration. He points out that the primary tradition of baseball is pastoral, more in the nature of a country fair than a city trade show. This does not suit our modern urban settings where domed stadiums feature manufactured weather, nonstop TV shows, and wall-to-wall carpeting. Our sports parks, like our shopping centers, become an indistinguishable feature of our urban landscape, where even our leisure reflects the values of speed and efficiency.

c. Use It Up

If you need something, find what works. If something doesn't work, fix it; if you're through with it, throw it out. In any case, let's get on with it, and don't waste my time. The pervasive influence of these attitudes is reflected even in what an object means in our culture. In an unpublished paper, Herbert Dreyfus borrowed a term from the later Heidegger to designate the way we deal with our surroundings. Things around us belong to a "standing reserve." When we need something we use it; if it breaks, we fix it or throw it out.

A typical example of what an object means in American culture is the styrofoam cup. It is extremely useful for keeping liquids hot or cold, but this function exhausts its value. When we are finished with it we throw it out (though, ironically, we are not "finished" with it since it remains as a serious and toxic pollutant to our environment). How very different, Dreyfus points out, is the Japanese teacup, which is preserved from generation to generation for its beauty and meaning. Even the way tea is taken in Japan reflects a complex of values unique to that culture; the tea ceremony is in fact a traditional art form. The cup is valued for its place in this web of values, rather than for its function alone. What this object means in Japan reflects more widely held values of delicacy, beauty, and tradition; in America, the values are efficiency and function. They in turn reflect deeper attitudes toward our place in the world.

It is not surprising, then, that consumption has come to be a central organizing principle of the American economy, and therefore for most individuals in America. Personal success as national progress is measured in terms of income and accumulation of things. John Kenneth Galbraith expressed his fear about this tendency some time ago:

> From a detached point of view, expansion in the output of many goods is not easily accorded a social purpose. More

cigarettes cause more cancer. More alcohol causes more cirrhosis. More automobiles cause more accidents, maiming and death; also more preemption of space for highways and parking; also more pollution of the air and the countryside. What is called a high standard of living consists, in considerable measure, in arrangements for avoiding muscular energy, increasing sensual pleasure and for enhancing caloric intake above any conceivable nutritional requirement. Nonetheless, the belief that increased production is a worthy social goal is very nearly absolute. . . . That social progress is identical with a rising standard of living has the aspect of a faith. (*The New Industrial State*, 164)

The Communication of the Gospel

Now we must ask how this setting will influence the way we hear and live out the gospel. Our ambiguity toward culture will play its role here as well. Americans are clearly socialized to place priority on doing and making, to define reality in material and objective terms. We should expect therefore that people will be interested to know how Christianity will be of use in their lives. This, of course, is exactly what we find. As in the case of social justice in Third World situations, Americans will need to see that Christianity can confront the basic issues they wrestle with and provide answers that carry weight. The history of Christianity in America, especially of the revivals, has been marked by a hunger for a faith that works, and it would be foolish to ignore this need for the practical.

The simple fact is that most Americans are not interested in hearing the gospel as a philosophical explanation of the world. But they *are* wrestling with family problems: how to encourage and protect teenagers, how to help young married children, and so on. Therefore, it is reasonable to suppose that they are interested in hearing how the gospel relates to these problems.

The Scriptures, after all, present the man and woman as having been given dominion over the created order. The material order has a positive value in creation and is endowed with the potential for development and growth. Because the world is a creation of God and because we are made stewards of it, we can explore and develop it. Moreover, it is an important component of the gospel message that God has entered this world order in Jesus Christ, and, with the pouring out of the Holy Spirit at Pentecost, intends to indwell and transform believers' lives. So we can quite properly speak of the actual impact of Christian truth on our lives.

But God's larger purposes suggest that technological discoveries are not only instruments of our own pleasure, but also are means to glorify God. The weaknesses inherent in American understanding of the material environment, with our boundless emphasis on potential and growth, is our neglect of inherent limitations that Scripture places on our dominion. Central to this is the account of Adam and Eve's disobedience to God's instructions. They were free to eat of every tree in the garden except the one in the center, a limitation on their freedom which they could not tolerate. The subsequent record makes clear that human fallenness leads people to exploit the created order and use it for perverted ends. Indeed, the single most important perversion is the denial of the larger divine purpose for our world, and our tendency to reduce its value to our immediate ends.

These remarks can be brought together in two observations about the relation between means and ends in American culture. Because of our unique history and geography, American middle-class culture has been almost entirely preoccupied with technical means divorced from questions of a final purpose and goal. A very important biblical principle says the purpose of our lives must be reflected in the means: behavior connotes purpose. But when means are divorced from ends, they are themselves treated as final goals. As Richard Bernstein notes in his discussion of John Dewey: "When we divorce the instrumental from the consummatory, ends frequently become indulgent dissipations, passive amusements, and distractions" (*John Dewey*, 154). Life itself becomes frivolous.

Even Christian means—evangelistic tools, Christian life seminars—when they are made ends in themselves, become banal and trivialize the gospel. Ironically, it may well be the success of Christianity in America which has blinded us to this fact.

But this leads to a second comment relating to means and ends. Preoccupation with means tends to obscure ends for which the means are not immediately obvious. It is hard for Americans to understand human life in any transcendent perspective, not because they are perverse or less intelligent than other people, but because they do not have vocabulary or terminology to discuss such ends. Americans are simply incapable of understanding how one might go about meeting a transcendent need. Since physical appetites are so immediately evident and so easily satisfied, it is easy to overlook emotional or spiritual appetites that are deeper and harder to satisfy. We are quite simply so busy fixing things (we have after all a lot of things to fix) that we overlook the plain fact that some things cannot be fixed. Some hungers cannot be satisfied by more self-indulgence.

In a word, this preoccupation with means carries an inherent danger of idolatry: that is, endowing the paraphernalia of life with final meaning. Home ownership, good education for our children, an annual vacation—these things are seen as rights which accrue to us as Americans. Indeed, we usually assume private ownership of resources is a right. But in the biblical view goods are not private property. Even if our labor makes them usable, they did not ultimately come from us. Goods receive their meaning from the social context both of their production and their consumption. These processes finally have their meaning in God's purposes for the human community and his creation.

At this point American culture provides a unique opening for the gospel. For it is becoming increasingly clear that affluence creates as many problems as it solves. Almost all of our major illnesses and social problems can be traced in one way or another to our affluent and indulgent lifestyle. The poignant question on the bumper sticker, "Are we having fun yet?," cannot be answered by another vacation in Europe. It is asking for something deeper and more comprehensive.

How then can the legitimate values of creation and the dynamic of growth be preserved, and at the same time people be convinced of their deep need for God? We must reflect on more of the American value system before we can propose any complete answer, but here we can point out the serious issue involved. Our emphasis on our material environment has blinded us to the social dimensions of our humanity. The pervading loneliness Americans experience may be an important point of entrance for the message of God's care and Jesus' love.

Christian Discipleship in the Virgin Land

When it comes to Christian discipleship in American society, one is more often struck by the unremarkable character of the Christian lifestyle. Clearly, Christians are very little different in lifestyle from their non-Christian neighbors. Our rushing around may be to committee meetings at church, but we are no less pressured and harried. Even our hymnody reflects these values: "I'm pressing on the upward way" . . . "Work for the night is coming." There seems to be very little of the quiet confidence that one would expect believers to exhibit. More often believers seem as driven and "backed up" as the people around them, even if the agenda is full of Christian things.

At the same time this has given American Christianity a vitality and strength for initiative in missions and evangelism. Why is it, I have often wondered, that Americans love to focus on the command to "go" into all the world, when in Matthew 28:19 this command is altogether missing in the Greek? I used to feel that this was because English translations improperly translate the verse as a command (as the KJV for example does). Now I think this is a good example of our culturally conditioned reading of Scripture. We Americans are always in motion; therefore it is a strong temptation to see missions as going somewhere. Since on the whole we like to travel, if missions has to do with travel, then we are interested. And so in missions and evangelism, we, like our secular neighbors in more pagan pursuits, confuse movement with progress.

In fact, of course, these verses are about making disciples: that is, bringing people to God and to each other. We know this, but even here we Americans are tempted to think in ways that are quantifiable: the number of people who have attended our meetings or responded to the invitation, the number of meetings or mailings, and so on. Notice what this practice implies. American Christians reflect the more general cultural tendency to interpret and evaluate goals (bringing people to God) in terms of the means used to reach that goal (meetings and mailings). This is strangely reminiscent of the problems we mentioned in our educational systems: educators currently are seeking to confront the crisis of goals (why are people in college at all?) in terms of means (give them all professional examinations before they graduate).

It may be that the gospel has a fresh message to address Americans that will restore a sense of place and meaning in their relation to the environment. It will give us again a sense of "world," a whole that belongs to God and is given to us in trust. But in giving back a sense of rootedness in God's good order, we may also experience afresh the anguish our rebellion has caused.

It is not surprising that it is our Southern writers who

have reminded us of the importance of this rootedness. Eudora Welty once said: "I am myself touched off by place. The place where I am and the place I know, and other places that familiarity with and love for my own make strange and lovely and enlightening to look into, are what set me to writing my stories" (in Woodward, *The Burden of Southern History*, 23-24). One thing the gospel will surely do is restore the blessed sense of being located, without encouraging us to endow physical places with ultimate meaning.

But it may also cause us to hear more clearly the cries of the dispossessed of the land, the victims of our obsession with progress. How often do we think, for example, of the way native Americans look upon the land?

> For each tribe of men Usen created, He also made a home. In the land for any particular tribe, He placed whatever would be best for the welfare of that tribe.
>
> When Usen created the Apaches, He also gave them homes in the West. He gave them such grain, fruits, and game as they needed to eat. . . . He gave them a pleasant climate, and all they needed for clothing and shelter was at hand.
>
> Thus it was in the beginning: the Apaches and their homes, each created for the other by Usen Himself. When they are taken from these homes, they sicken and die. (Meredith, *The Native American Factor*, 16)

Could it be that we have focused so exclusively on dominion and control that we have lost sight of other biblical emphases of cooperation and interrelationship? Part of the process of growth for American Christians will certainly involve hearing these other voices.

Robert Indiana, *DEMUTH AMERICAN DREAM #5*, 1962
(used by permission of the Art Gallery of Ontario, Toronto)

CHAPTER FOUR

The American Dream

THE FIRST PERSON TO REFER TO THE AMERICAN DREAM IN A serious study was probably James T. Adams writing in 1931. He quotes a young Russian immigrant, Mary Antin, who extols the joys of the Boston Public Library:

> This is my latest home, and it invites me to a glad new life. . . . My spirit is not tied to the monumental past, any more than my feet were bound to my grandfather's house below the hill. The past was only my cradle, and now it cannot hold me, because I am grown too big. . . . No! It is not I that belong to the past, but the past that belongs to me. America is the youngest of the nations, and inherits all that went before in history. And I am the youngest of America's children, and into my hands is given all her priceless heritage, to the last white star espied through the telescope, to the last great thought of the philosopher. Mine is the whole majestic past, and mine is the shining future. (416-17)

Here is a classic expression of what we are taught to feel about America: the future is always bright with promise, the past something to be outgrown and discarded. All of life is believed to favor the boundless optimism of especially the young and innocent. It is an incessant project: the America that fires our individual imagination is something we are pressed to engage in together; it is something new, a present full of possibilities and hope.

But problems arise in this mythological land of promise. The past is given no intrinsic value, outside of its preparation for today. As a result, evil and tragedy have no place; we certainly are not responsible for them. If they marked our past, it was simply because America was not ready to take her proud place in the world. Now things will be better.

In this chapter, we will assess the fundamental optimism of the American character, noting its sources, strengths, and weaknesses. First we must recognize that we are not talking about ideas that Americans hold as much as feelings we harbor about ourselves. In fact, when we articulate our attitudes, we often do not recognize them, just as most of us are shocked at the sound of our own voice. Though attitudes obviously contain cognitive elements, they are primarily an affective reaction to the world and to life. We may put it this way: Americans are temperamentally optimistic.

We examine the roots of this under three headings: the Puritan City of God; the Eschatology of the Revolution; and the Revival Mentality.

The Puritan City of God

While still aboard the *Arbella* en route to the New World, Governor John Winthrop highlighted what the founding of the Massachusetts colony meant for the colonists:

> We must not content ourselves with usual ordinary means. Whatsoever we did or ought to have done when we lived in England, the same must we do, and more also where we go. . . .
>
> Neither must we think that the Lord will bear with such

failings at our hands as He doth from those among whom we have lived. . . .

Thus stands the cause between God and us: we are entered into covenant with Him for this work; we have taken out a commission, the Lord hath given us leave to draw our own articles. . . .

We shall find that the God of Israel is among us. . . . For we must consider that we shall be as a city upon a hill, the eyes of all people are upon us. (In Ahlstrom, *Religious History*, 146-47)

Two elements of the Puritan project were articulated in this famous sermon. First was the conviction that God by a "special over-ruling providence" (ibid.) was bringing them to inaugurate a new period of history. Central to this, of course, was the Old Testament concept of covenant. In the words of John Preston, a Puritan divine writing in 1629, this was the great mercy that "the glorious God of heaven and earth should be willing to enter into Covenant, that he should be willing to indent with us, as it were, that he should be willing to make himself a debtor to us" (*The New Covenant*, 330-31).

They were therefore the New Israel setting out in the providence of God to form a holy commonwealth, an example to all the world of God's goodness and grace. Looking to Scripture as the higher law, they set about reforming the institutions of their society by God's will. This confidence in both their calling and the resources available to them unleashed a creative energy that greatly influenced our political and educational institutions. This is surely an important source for our American conception of voluntarism: that people working together can solve the problems that confront them. It was also an important encouragement to individual initiative.

But Winthrop's sermon implies something else. The challenge thrown out to this unusual congregation is this: we must do better than any have done before us, and if we do not, we cannot expect God to bear with our failings. One of the attitudinal paradoxes present at the birth of our country is this combination of God's providence and our responsibility in this project. One of the ways this appeared was in people being allowed to choose their own ministers. Herbert Schneider notes that "the theocracy was, from the point of view of the elect, both in theory and practice an assertion of liberty and democracy" (*The Puritan Mind*, 30). At the same time God was choosing them, they were busy choosing for themselves; here the "vox populi" was literally the "vox dei." This combination surely has something to do with the confident activism that marked the settlers' attitude toward life.

But it is this very confidence that had important consequences in our American story. First, because God had specially chosen these people to form a holy nation, any opposition to their project was believed to be an attack of Satan on God's work. Whether from without—in the attacks from the Indians—or from within, in the ominous witchcraft or the rebellion of Roger Williams, the devil was seeking to oppose the work of God. Very few people today believe that America is God's chosen people, but many have learned to see the struggles both within and without as between light and darkness. Attacks on America are attacks, if not on God, at least on the sacred cause of liberty. "Only in the United States," writes Sacvan Bercovitch, "has nationalism carried with it the Christian meaning of the sacred" (*American Jeremiad*, 176).

A second consequence follows from the heightened sense of responsibility leaders like Winthrop placed on the people. No student of Christian history is surprised to see that the Puritans' early zeal gave way by the second generation to compromise. One of the ways personal responsibility was manifested was the requirement, instituted in 1635, that each church member narrate his conversion experience before being admitted to full membership. This internalizing of the American project was to have far-reaching consequences, as we will see. But its most immediate effect was to exclude many of the second generation from full communion. This led, in 1662, to the halfway covenant, wherein the second generation was allowed to remain in the church but was not permitted to take the Lord's Supper.

This expedient may have solved some doctrinal issues, but it could not hide the fact that the Puritans were not acting like the holy people they set out to be. Preachers began to make generous use of prophetic texts in which God through his prophet lamented the failure of Israel to be a holy nation. This attack by one New England clergyman is typical:

> Why was it that "no place under heaven . . . will so highly provoke and incense the displeasure of God as . . . New England?" Why were there "*no persons in all the world unto whom God speaketh as he doth unto us* [by His] . . . most awful Providences?" The reason was obvious. Because New England was God's country, its inhabitants must expect His lash. "*God is terrible out of his holy places.*" (Quoted by Bercovitch, *American Jeremiad*, 57)

These jeremiads featured prominently in the history of this period. As Sacvan Bercovitch has pointed out, something significant was happening to our national character—especially, he believes, for what later became middle-class attitudes. These people had failed to live up to their high calling; therefore they had earned God's displeasure. Here is the other side of this incredible sense of mission: the Puritans not only had the feeling of being a people sent on a mission, but they shared a corporate sense of failure when they failed in that mission. The Puritans had such high expectations for what America was supposed to do and be that disillusionment and breast-beating early on became something of a national style.

It is clear that we have never quite lost our sense of being on a mission, of being people on the cutting edge. And when we fail in this mission, we share a corporate guilt. Of course this mission has long since become a purely secular affair; the major step in that process we must examine next.

The Revolution: Secular Events with a Sacred Telos

The Puritans had the sense that America was perhaps humanity's last chance to show God's mercy before the end of history. This habit of viewing contemporary events as the birth pangs of the millennial age was to become influential throughout American history. It was especially evident in the American Revolution.

Though there is much debate on details, the immediate preparation for the revolt of the colonies was the First Great Awakening of the 1730s and 40s. Alan Heimert has characterized this as a watershed in American history. He notes, "From 1740 on, American thought and expression—or, more precisely, that of the evangelical American—was above all characterized by a note of expectation" ("Great Awakening as Watershed," 127).

This thesis has been subjected to a great deal of clarification since Heimert wrote these words. It is now clear that Jonathan Edwards' closest followers were generally indifferent to the Revolution (though there were exceptions). Like their descendants in the 20th century, these Christians were more concerned about personal salvation than about political events. For example, Joseph Bellamy, one of the most famous of these, said in 1775: "My desire and my prayer to God is, that my son Jonathan may be saved. And then, whatever happens to America . . . this year or next, you will be happy forever" (In Noll, Hatch, and Marsden, *Search for Christian America*, 57).

Moreover, the real heirs to the Puritan ideas of the Holy Commonwealth were not the new light revivalists, but the old lights who opposed it. The old lights felt that God's purposes were now to be fulfilled in the events of contemporary history. But even for these, the events of the Awakening were significant as the first truly national event: the colonies began to see themselves for the first time as a people (ibid.: 53ff.).

Above all, the revivals created an air of expectation that history was moving to a new and perhaps final stage. Moreover, it was the categories of biblical eschatology that were exploited to articulate these hopes. The postmillennial theology of Edwards and his followers was particularly compatible with these fresh hopes. It "had the effect of teaching many Americans to expect some coming perfection of history, achieved by progressive stages, to which contemporary events, first the Awakening and later the Revolution, must be the prelude" (James F. Maclear, "The Republic and the Millennium," 184).

Since this period is critical to our history and the story we are following, it is important we understand this carefully. The revivalists saw the freedom of the coming kingdom in terms of freedom from sin. The sense of sin which Edwards and his colleagues inherited from the Puritans has become proverbial; indeed, it has become a maligned part of the Puritan caricature precisely because we have lost its sense of limitation and evil. But for them the expectation of what God could do with the American people was closely tied to the freedom from individual and corporate sin which the revivals were making possible.

Bellamy's letter about his son reflects the disillusionment the exponents of revival felt when society did not immediately undergo a national conversion. In fact, the decline of church attendance that began early in the century continued inexorably in spite of the Awakenings (see *Search for Christian America*, 54).

How then did the Revolution come to be identified so frequently with the millennial program of God? Nathan Hatch has pointed out that in the more liberal Congregational New England clergymen began consistently identifying the project of defeating the British with the millennial work of God. The Revolution became quite simply the apocalyptic history of God; the millennium was thus secularized. "By 1760 New England clergymen appeared to have lost a clear distinction between the Kingdom of God and the goals of their own political program" (Hatch, *The Sacred Cause of*

Liberty, 43). The ideal they sought was no longer a holy people (remember these clergymen were generally opposed to the revivals), but civil and religious liberty, what was often called "the sacred cause of liberty."

Ironically, these political ideas were inherited from the very British they were fighting, from a tradition historians call the "real whig" political tradition (cf. Noll, "Humanistic Values"). As this tradition was reinterpreted, hope lay in the expulsion of the British, the incarnate powers of evil. The assumption was that what impeded the great American project was this corrupt and arbitrary power threatening from without. The colonists freed from this yoke would surely produce the flowers of liberty.

What is interesting is the prominent role preachers played in creating the language that would express the values of revolt. As with the Puritans, history from these pulpits was still seen as a cosmic struggle, but now it was between the good colonies and the bad British, rather than between God and the devil. Perry Miller sums up this period: "The revolutionary divines, in their zeal for liberty, committed themselves unwittingly to the proposition that in this case the expulsion of the British would automatically leave America a pure society" ("From Covenant to Revival," 154-55). Miller in fact believes it was in this tradition of preaching, rather than in reaction to Deism and the Enlightenment, that the roots of the Second Great Awakening lay.

But before we turn to this part of the story, we note the persistence of the sense of mission and the boundless confidence in what America could accomplish, once freed from what was perceived as arbitrary power. There was something noble in this. In contrast to Europe, where God was often allied with oppressive and traditional forces, here he was clearly on the side of freedom. Henry May writes: "In America, Providence, and specifically Christian and Calvinist Providence, was on the side of the people" (*Ideas, Faiths, and Feelings*, 143).

But now a new political element was added to the American mission. For the first time the colonies were actually playing a role in the community of nations. With the Puritan and biblical heritage, the temptation was great to make a direct political application of the language of divine calling and millennial expectation. Most people doing this had lost all sense of God's personal involvement in human affairs, or even of the real meaning of God's intervention at the end of history. But they inherited the sense of expectation and the sense of mission, as well as the idea that history displayed the great struggle between good and evil. These had passed from items of explicit faith into the tacit values of the American character. Before we assess the significance of this complex of values, we turn to the events of the 19th century.

The Revival Mentality

As in the 1740s, the revivals that swept both the frontier and the settled eastern seaboard in the first decade of the 19th century raised the expectation that "a wondrous new age was aborning and that the systematic labors of the saints would help bring it to pass" (Moorhead, "Between Progress and Apocalypse," 527). This special destiny was given characteristic expression in 1830 by President Francis Wayland of Brown University before the Sunday School Union. "Why stand we here all the day idle?" he wanted to know,

> [When] a revival of piety may be witnessed in every neighbourhood throughout the land; the principles of the Gospel may be made to regulate the detail of individual and national intercourse; and high praises of God may be heard from every habitation; and perhaps before the youth of this generation be gathered to their fathers, there may burst forth upon these highly-favored States the light of Millennial Glory. What is to prevent it? ... I do believe that the option is put into our hands. It is for us . . . to say, whether the present religious movement shall be onward,

until it terminate in the universal triumph of the Messiah, or whether all shall go back again. . . . The church has for two thousand years been praying "Thy kingdom come." Jesus Christ is saying unto us, "It shall come if you desire it." (In James F. Maclear, 188-89)

The same combination of attitudes we noted in Winthrop's sermon are present here. Here is the sense of God's special providence being manifest in this place and time; here too is the challenge to be involved in God's program. Indeed, it appears that it is up to human will whether this proves to be the time of the Messiah's appearing. Added to these elements now is the special ingredient that the revolutionary period introduced: these states are bearers of God's special program. But what gave Wayland his special confidence that all this might be true? To what evidence could he appeal?

He might have pointed to two effects of the Great Awakening which were obvious to any careful observer. First was the incredible impetus given to social reform. As Timothy Smith has convincingly demonstrated, the revivals and the perfectionist aspirations they spawned were the "drive shaft of social reform" (*Revivalism and Social Reform*, 8). In particular, it was the voluntary principle that was the means for major innovations in American society. After the revivals, George Marsden notes wryly, every vice of society seemed to have a corresponding society to stamp it out (*The Evangelical Mind*, 15ff.). Of course missionary and evangelistic societies were the most prominent, but there were also societies against liquor, gambling, slavery, and so on.

Put differently, the hope engendered by the revivals issued in the particularly American hunger for a Christianity that would "work." As Timothy Smith comments: "The quest for perfection joined with compassion for poor and needy sinners and a rebirth of millennial expectation to make popular Protestantism a mighty social force" (149). This of course speaks of the "can do" mentality we examined in the last chapter, but also of the unique optimism that our problems are amenable to a sustained and systematic approach that is leading us to a new and better day. This in turn rested on the millennial vision of a righteous society which God was bringing about in this land.

But this optimism about social problems was closely related to a second equally significant product of the revival period: what might be called "immediatism." Though the literature on this is not as extensive as on voluntarism, David Brion Davis defines it as an attitude of directness, of forthrightness that derives from an underlying moral claim ("The Emergence of Immediatism," 237). Clearly, the source of this moral impetus is the revivals, though the natural rights philosophy of the 18th century was also influential.

But nothing in the 18th-century gradualism could account for this sense that things could be changed dramatically, and all at once. Partly, the underlying moral claim that Davis points to is this: sin cannot be tolerated. It must be excised in a radical way. Also involved was the romantic need to liberate inner moral forces. But most significant is the dominance of revivals in the West and the East, and the many testimonies of changed lives, which created what might be called an expectation for revival—the sense that things which were wrong could be changed not someday, but now. This language has become so common that we do not pause to reflect on its parentage. From the "freedom now" slogans of the Civil Rights Movement to the immediatism evident in our half hour television programs, we have come to believe that all problems are subject to quick solutions.

Not surprisingly, as Davis points out, it was attitudes like this that finally forced the showdown of the war between the states. Despite the fact that this was the most savage war that this innocent nation had known, most observers did not question the basic optimistic attitudes that we have been describing. Indeed, by mid-century millennial hopes were again being uncritically fused with political hopes for America, with new influence from the cult of progress (see James Maclear, 187 and Bob Goudzwaard, *Capitalism and Progress,* 79). These attitudes continued to grow right up to the end of the century. The Civil War was merely history clearing its throat.

It is likely that the progressive movement from 1889-1920 had its roots in the same revivalist view of conversion. Robert Crunden documents the fact that many progressives were raised in conservative Protestant homes. Most of them, he notes, came to doubt the role of God in human affairs, but they maintained the mechanism of conversion, oriented now to the goals of social reform (*Ministers of Reform*, 16).

Josiah Strong can once again be taken as typical when he says in 1885: "For if this generation is faithful to its trust, America is to become God's right arm in his battle with the world's ignorance and oppression and sin" (*Our Country*, 253-54). Grant Wacker summarizes the situation at the end of the century by noting that both liberal and higher-life theologians shared the zealous, essentially optimistic spirit of the age. He cites "the zealousness of the [higher-life] movement's leaders to reclaim souls and to reform society at home and abroad. The sheer magnitude of their efforts is persuasive evidence that premillennialism was not an ideology of despair but an efficient instrument for mobilizing religious energies" ("The Holy Spirit and the Spirit of the Age," 58). For both parties, and even for those outside the church, the widespread desire for renewal was a general cultural impulse (ibid.: 62).

But it would be misleading to leave the impression that all impetus for hope and optimism was religious in origin during the 19th century. For transcendentalism was a parallel source for attitudes which we have been describing. There was one area where the revival did not encourage uncritical optimism: its view of individual sin. For revivalists and their theologian colleagues at Andover and Princeton, the reality of inherited sin was the fundamental human problem. This led Ralph Waldo Emerson to distinguish his party of hope from the revivalist party of memory. Though the revivals and the immediatism we have examined encouraged their own denial of history, Emerson felt the party of hope must only look forward. Brooding darkly over the past, he felt, had no value in creating a hopeful future.

In 1837 Emerson addressed the Beta Kappa Society at Cambridge, in what has been called the "literary Declaration of Independence." It is time, he proclaimed, that we look to ourselves for creative inspiration, and not to Europe or Greece. "I ask not for the great, the remote, the romantic; what is doing in Italy or Arabia; what is Greek art, or Provençal minstrelsy; I embrace the common, I explore and sit at the feet of the familiar, the low. Give me insight into to-day, and you may have the antique and future worlds" (*Essays*, 102).

Hope in this view of things rests not on what God will do or has done, but in what the individual can do. Moreover, the present takes on a kind of imperialism over both past and future. This recurring hostility against the past appears often in our history, but the most colorful exponent is the young reformer Holgrave, in Hawthorne's novel *House of Seven Gables* (1851). He echoes Emerson:

> Shall we never, never get rid of this Past? . . . It lies upon the Present like a giant's dead body! In fact, the case is just as if a young giant were compelled to waste all his strength in carrying about the corpse of the old giant, his grand-father, who died a long while ago, and only needs to be decently buried. Just think a moment, and it will startle you to see what slaves we are to bygone times — to Death, if we give the matter the right word! (162)

One could not have a clearer expression of so much American hostility, not only to the past in general, but to old people in particular. It seems that freedom for the future can only be bought at the price of a decisive break with the past. Here is a very different kind of immediatism, one that rests not on the intervention of God, but on the sovereignty of the living individual.

In Emerson and his colleagues a major change in the American character is taking place. Hope and memory, always in tension in American history, are definitively split apart. Hope is now made to rest on itself, rather than on faith in God or even historical developments. R. W. B. Lewis notes "the ancient theological virtue of hope (which rested on faith in God) was transformed into the human quality of hopefulness (which rested on faith in the heroic American)" (*The American Adam,* 175). This explains how Thoreau could celebrate each morning on Walden Pond as though it brought a new life:

> Every morning was cheerful invitation to make my life of equal simplicity, and I may say innocence, with Nature. . . . I got up early and bathed in the pond; that was a religious exercise, and one of the best things which I did. They say that characters were engraven on the bathing tub of King Tching-thang to this effect: "Renew thyself completely each day; do it again, and again, and forever again." I can understand that. Morning brings back the heroic ages. . . . There was something cosmical about it; a standing advertisement, till forbidden, of the everlasting vigor and fertility of the world. The morning, which is the most memorable season of the day, is the awakening hour. (*Walden,* 79-80)

This flower of hope, however severed from the roots that had nourished it, continued its influence in American culture. Without it the whole progressive era would not have been possible This movement, arguably the final fruit of New England theology, assumes innocence and hope: there is a special calling for this nation that gives us moral space to be optimistic about our future. We believe in America; therefore we have hope. It is fitting to close this survey with perhaps the most famous of the progressives, the one Bruce Kuklick calls the last of the New England theologians: John Dewey. In his book *A Common Faith* (1934) he sought to express many of the values of the party of hope. He wrote:

> Were men and women actuated throughout the length and breadth of human relations with the faith and ardor that have at times marked historic religions the consequences

would be incalculable. . . . But religions have attempted something similar, directed moreover toward a less promising object—the supernatural. It does not become those who hold that faith may move mountains to deny in advance the possibility of its manifestation on the basis of verifiable realities. There already exists, though in a rudimentary form, the capacity to relate social conditions and events to their causes, and the ability will grow with exercise. . . . It remains to weld all these things together. (80-81)

Reading these buoyant words, one might never know that World War I had brought about the breakup of the patriotic progressive movement. One famous commentator in fact dared to call such sentiments "platitudinous." Reinhold Niebuhr, writing in his *Moral Man and Immoral Society* (1932), dismissed Dewey's hopefulness as unreal, based on an analysis that "has no clear counsels about the way to overcome social inertia" (xiv; and see Fox, *Reinhold Niebuhr*, 136).

The hope that Dewey expresses not even Niebuhr could snuff out; it springs eternal in the American breast. Indeed in our century, though it has lost its corporate dimension, this hope has become the driving force behind the quest for individual fulfillment. So it is appropriate that Dewey writes about the same time as Adams' Russian immigrant girl rhapsodizes about her future in America. For both express a fundamental impulse of the American character. It is an impulse that was present from the first reflections of the Puritans about what God was doing in the New World. Something new is happening in this place and all the world will look here for inspiration.

Conclusion: Communicating the Gospel to Optimists

William A. Clebsch in his book *From Sacred to Profane America* writes about the paradox of the success of religion in America. All the battles which religion won—in education, morality, and welfare—and passed on to the wider society were won at the expense of the religious character of these battles. Our discussion has already suggested that this view of secularization may be oversimplified, but in this case the evidence suggests Clebsch is right: values that had their origin in religious belief have now passed into general currency among people who rarely think of God. The final irony, however, is that this very hopefulness has now become, for many people, an obstacle to genuine faith in Christ.

The first thing to recognize is that the new thing history promises has its roots only in the biblical God who intervenes in history. As Mircea Eliade notes, "Practically all the non-European cultures are without historic consciousness, and even if they have a traditional historiography—as in the case of China, or the countries under Islamic culture—its function is always to provide exemplary models" (*Myths, Dreams and Mysteries*, 235). Moreover, the appearance of the new thing in biblical history has no parallel in Ancient Near Eastern, or later in the Greek, cultures.

Equally important, however, is the fact that biblically the new thing that God is doing in history is nowhere associated with the settlement of Israel in the land or indeed with any specific political project, but appears first in the prophets in the promise of future saving activity (see Jer. 31:31ff.). In the New Testament this new intervention is tied specifically to the work of Christ and the new covenant he inaugurates with his death (Luke 22:20), which is also called a new creation (in Gal. 6:15). This reality, which is now manifested by the pouring out of the Holy Spirit, is meant to spread its influence over all nations (Matt. 28:19-21), with the church as Christ's body challenging injustice wherever it appears (see 2 Cor. 5:17). Clearly the church will play a political role, but this role is now universalized. God's concern is now with all the nations, and not any particular people or group of people.

At the same time we must recognize how important this openness to the future and this faith in the new have been for our understanding of Christianity. The American sense that history is open makes it possible to speak of God doing something new for a community or an individual. That our theological language quite appropriately reflects this can be seen in this quotation from Dietrich Bonhoeffer:

> If we would follow Jesus we must take certain definite steps. The first step, which follows the call, cuts the disciple off from his previous existence. The call to follow at once produces a new situation. . . . [S]ince [Jesus] is the Christ, he must make it clear from the start that his word is not an abstract doctrine, but the re-creation of the whole life of man. The call to follow implies that there is only one way of believing on Jesus Christ, and that is by leaving all and going with the incarnate Son of God. (*The Cost of Discipleship*, 52)

This language is very congenial to American ways of thinking, as is the language of personal decision that involves a break with family and friends. José Míguez Bonino speaks of the way this has influenced Christianity in Latin America:

> Preaching emphasizes the elimination of all "social mediations": "you stand alone before Christ"; "you have to decide for yourself." Eternal life and eternal death hang on the outcome of this moment of decision. In a way, immigrants or peasants who have migrated to the city—anonymous members of the new subproletariat—are thus challenged, perhaps for the first time, to take in hand their own destiny. Clearly we find ourselves here in the world of the "free individual" of modern society. (*Toward a Christian Political Ethics*, 60)

As Míguez goes on to note, this has more clearly reflected the culture of the sending countries than either the biblical message or the needs of Latin America.

Why have Americans focused on being "born again" as the dominant image of the Christian life? Why are we called "born again" Christians rather than, say, "people of the way," when the first is mentioned only once in the New Testament and the second often (see John 14:6; Acts 9:12; 19:9; 24:22 et al.)? Surely this has much to do with the deep-seated American need for novelty and for the hope offered by a new life.

Yet there is clearly something admirable in all of this. Where, after all, does the ability to dream come from? In African cultures dreams are a unique gift of God. Though we are speaking of very different kinds of dreams—indeed, Puritan culture was highly suspicious of dreams and revelations—it is well to recognize that the ability to dream of new possibilities, of a future that is filled with hope, is a special gift of God and one that is consistent in many ways with the teaching of Scripture. A sign of the age of the Spirit is that "young men shall see visions, and . . . old men shall dream dreams" (Acts 3:17). If God is free and he is good, something special can happen to his people today. It is not hard to see why the language of victorious Christianity has become the primary language of evangelicalism, or why our most famous evangelistic tool begins like this: God loves you and has a wonderful plan for your life.

We have argued that we need to distinguish between using the cultural forms to communicate the gospel and allowing the Word of God to transform these forms as God's people move toward maturity. Hope is a wonderful gift, and where it exists it can be used to point people to the source of that hope. But when people begin to follow Christ, they must learn that discipleship involves a bearing of the cross— sharing the pain and brokenness of the fallen order. This involves memory as well as hope.

For without an informed memory of our past, and what God has done with that past, our openness to the future is ultimately without direction. If hope means simply that anything can happen, it can also mean that tragedy or disaster is possible, or that life may after all be intractable. In the end memory is the basis of real hope. As Kathleen Fischer argues, "The stories of the past reveal to us the possibilities of the present. God's call takes account of where we are and always invites us to further growth. In following that call, then, we need to know who we have become" (*The Inner Rainbow*, 104).

But memory is important for a further reason. What if, after all, we do not succeed? What if, after setting out with the best hope in the world, we fail. What then? The other side of our irrepressible hope, as we have seen, is disillusionment. Perhaps the deep cynicism among certain segments of our society—our teenage suicides, or our drug culture—is simply the dark side of our cultural hopefulness. When the dream is not fulfilled, there is nothing to live for. Robert Indiana captures this tension in his striking "Demuth American Dream #5," reproduced at the beginning of this chapter. There, in the flashing shapes of the neon lights, are pleas to indulge—"eat," "hug"—but also warnings about our frailty—"err," "die." How do these fit together? As Christopher Lasch noted not long ago, a sense of ending pervades Western civilization (*The Culture of Narcissism*, 18-19). For those who have experienced this darkness, the message that God wants to do something new may sound hollow.

Where can we go to find a language to express the reality of suffering and death, of loss of hope in our culture in a way that does not lead to cynicism? This may be the most important question about contextualization that American Christians can ask themselves. Here is a point at which we might well listen to other voices, those who have paid a heavy price for our cheerful optimism.

A good place to begin this search, at another point in our history, is our own Civil War. Then it became clear to both sides that unity and liberty must be bought with a terrible price. Abraham Lincoln put it like this in his second inaugural address: "Yet, if God wills that [this war] continue, until all the wealth piled by the bond-man's two hundred and fifty years of unrequited toil shall be sunk, and until every drop of blood drawn with the lash, shall be paid by another drawn with the sword, as was said three thousand years ago, so still it must be said 'the judgments of the Lord, are true and righteous altogether'" (reprinted in *Voices from the Heart*,

Lundin and Noll, p. 175). Here is a major American figure at a pivotal point in our history, employing the language of suffering and sacrifice. He voices here an awareness that has survived primarily among people living in the South, who bore the brunt of defeat, occupation, and reconstruction (see Woodward, *Burden of Southern History*). For these the Civil War was more than an accident of history; it was a reflection of something essential about the fallen world. It is not surprising that this part of our country has alone been able to produce writers like Flannery O'Connor and William Faulkner who can portray believable evil.

In general, Americans do not like this message of darkness—it seems depressing. Perhaps we have a respect for people who understand the place of suffering in the world. But I wonder if the Lincoln we remember is not another Lincoln altogether. Perhaps he is the boy who overcame great odds to become president, who rose from a log cabin to the White House.

But there is another group of people in our country who have suffered from the price of America's progress—the black Americans. Their literature features suffering and bondage; their songs call for the release that is found only in death ("fly away to Jesus"). On August 28, 1963, Martin Luther King, Jr., spoke out of this tradition from the steps of the Lincoln Memorial. While huge crowds surged around him, he recalled the promise of both Lincoln and the founders of our country: "One hundred years . . . [after Lincoln's proclamation], the Negro lives on a lonely island of poverty in the midst of a vast ocean of material prosperity." The architects of our republic, he went on, issued us all a promissory note "that all men would be guaranteed the unalienable rights of life, liberty, and the pursuit of happiness. . . . It is obvious today that America has defaulted on this promissory note. . . . But we refuse to believe the bank of justice is bankrupt." Then, abandoning his prepared speech, he spoke those prophetic lines: "I still have a dream. It is a dream deeply rooted in the American dream . . . that my four little children will one day live in a nation where they will not be judged by the color of their skin but by the content of their character" (in Oates, *Let the Trumpet Sound*, 259-61). But his most important line is seldom quoted, and it comes to us from his biblical faith: "I still believe that somehow the unearned suffering of the blacks is redemptive."

Here is a genuine echo of biblical hope—not based on the fact of our being a chosen people but on the reality that God's ear is open to the cries of people who suffer. What is at stake here is very important to our conception of the gospel. An important biblical theme, seen for example in the Magnificat of Luke, is that God's deliverance comes to those in a position of need, not to those in a position of privilege. Though the wealthy of this world know the goodness of God and the blessing of creation, a focus on the goodness of creation alone leads to emptiness, and not to hope (see Ecclesiastes). Moreover, the comfortable are seldom moved to call out to God in need, and so they see no need to repent. Suffering alone does not earn God's grace, but it does make us feel our need and often moves us to call on God for grace and forgiveness. Of course, without repentance there can be no lasting experience of God's grace; but to repent is, in part at least, to recognize failure and need.

Americans are a people with an ethos of privilege, not an ethos of need. We are imbued with the expectation of success, not an awareness of failure. This means we not only cannot deal well with suffering and death, but that we dangerously misinterpret the gospel. For in it the way to life must always be through death, and without the realization of failure and inability we cannot have hope for the future. Indeed, without these we cannot know God. Again, the irony of the biblical story is that in a fallen world real hope comes only through death. Perhaps from dialogue with that other American tradition, and with these other voices of Scripture, we will not only attract unbelievers with the promise of the abundant life, but will ourselves be moved toward maturity with the call to fill up the sufferings of Christ.

Roy Lichtenstein, *MR. BELLAMY*, 1961
(used by permission of the Fort Worth Art Museum)

CHAPTER FIVE

The American Adam

So Narcissus went on his cruel way, a scorner of love. But at last one of those he wounded prayed a prayer and it was answered by the gods: "May he who loves not others love himself." The great goddess Nemesis, which means righteous anger, undertook to bring this about. As Narcissus bent over a clear pool for a drink and saw there his own reflection, on the moment he fell in love with it. "Now I know," he cried, "what others have suffered from me, for I burn with love of my own self—and yet how can I reach that loveliness I see mirrored in the water? But I cannot leave it. Only death can set me free." And so it happened. He pined away, leaning perpetually over the pool, fixed in one long gaze.

In Edith Hamilton, *Mythology*, 115.

THE PURITANS SAW THE SETTLING OF AMERICA AS THE FIRST-fruits of the end times. But the arena in which this drama of hope was to be played out was the individual soul. In this of course they reflected a long Christian tradition, stretching back through Luther and Augustine to the Apostle Paul. It was Paul who made the reality of "Christ in the believer" the functional equivalent of the kingdom of God. Though he nowhere denied the public impact of faith, he made the locus of spiritual life God's Spirit "bearing witness with our spirit" (Rom. 8:16).

But the definitive influence on Western spirituality was St. Augustine, especially in his autobiography. There life with God is the inward quest of the soul for reality, and its struggle with its own evil desires. "Therefore," the Bishop of Hippo concluded, "is my soul like a land where no water is, because as it cannot itself enlighten itself, so can it not of itself satisfy itself. For so is the fountain of life with Thee, like as in Thy light we shall see light" (*Confessions*, 279).

Luther added the moral dimension to the medieval mystical quest: the search for the approval of a righteous God. The question "where do I find a righteous God?" found its answer in the drama of the soul coming to rest in God's goodness.

All of this is so familiar to American evangelicals that we overlook that this represents not only the roots of our view of faith, but an important source for the way middle-class Americans in general reflect on their experience of life. This spiritual individualism provided at least a framework and language that Americans came to use to describe their experience. An equally significant influence is the Enlightenment view of the person, and its impact on the American character. We examine these influences in four settings: the Puritan conversion narrative; the rights of man; 19th-century "perfectionism"; and, in our century, client-centered counseling.

The Puritan Conversion Narrative

The unique characteristic of the Puritans, notes Sacvan Bercovitch, was the attempt to transmute history into the drama of every soul (*Puritan Origins*, 7). He goes on to note that the

Puritan conception of Christianity was the reliving of the life of Christ in the individual's experience, what they called so appropriately the "*application* of Christ" (13). This is not to say that Puritans believed faith was equivalent to contemplation. On the contrary, this applying of Christ was to take place in action and personal experience in the world. But it was appropriated personally and individually. As Patricia Caldwell explains it, the Puritan conviction held that "the better the man, the more continually he lives on a knife edge in an endless process of wayfaring and warfaring, a ceaseless testing by the vicissitudes of life" (*The Puritan Conversion Narrative*, 15-16).

The personal testimony of conversion had long been important, but it was not until 1635 that it became a requirement for church membership in New England. As we noticed in the preceding chapter, before formal admission to the body of believers every person had to testify publicly in front of the congregation. The assumption was that what was significant for faith must take place within the personal experience of each person. Moreover, this experience had to be publicly shared, and when it was it would "ring true" to the assembled believers. Thomas Hooker explained the value of this:

> The soul . . . hath an inward work, which, though happily he cannot discover the manner and order thereof, nor expresse it to others, yet he knows more thereof than any man under heaven. . . . There is in a Saint of God an inward tenderness of affection, a leaning of his soul towards God which no man knowes but he that hath it. (In ibid.: 91-92)

What is striking for our purposes is the universality of this requirement. This was not only for elders or ministers, but for all members. If all were members by virtue of their personal encounter with God, so the assumption goes, we must hear from them all. The experience of each one was vital, and they must each have their say. This portion from a testimony of "Brother Jackson's maid" is typical:

So feeling many sins and hearing Jeremiah 18—is there no balm in Gilead—showed reason why we lie in our wants because there is balm in Gilead. We go not to Christ. So I went on. . . . And after this the Lord sent affliction and frightened me with death. And being in trouble, I knew not what to do though I had prayed and read and frequented ordinances. And so, that affliction was continued and so I prayed to God to add to my days that I might live to make my calling sure. (In ibid.: 169)

The project of the "New Israel" which we described in the last chapter was a central obsession of the Puritan imagination, but it was bound up with "each person's notion of, hope for, and recapitulation of his or her own experience of salvation" (ibid.: 26). The point is not that this experience of faith became normative in the American experience, but that the need for personal expression and testimony became, in Bercovitch's words, the rhetoric of American identity. We will see that the content and object of faith were soon discarded, but the importance of individual expression continued. As Bercovitch summarizes: "Early New England rhetoric provided a ready framework for inverting later secular values—human perfectibility, technological progress, democracy . . . —into the mold of sacred teleology" (*Puritan Origins*, 136). Patricia Caldwell adds that one must look here for the beginnings of American literature. She sees the dialectic that developed there between expectation and disenchantment as characteristic of American literature. In these Puritan narratives we find "some of the first faint murmurings of a truly American voice, emerging from little-known, ordinary people in community who, during a few decades in our history, tried to act on the idea that their lives were worth writing—or talking—about" (41).

The Rights of Man

We have seen that during the Revolutionary War the essentially religious goal of history became a secular and political quest. A parallel process affected the view of the individual with, if anything, even more far-reaching results. This process was defined by two interrelated beliefs, one relating to history, the other to the individual.

During the last half of the 18th century, the sense of God's immediate involvement and his providential ordering was rapidly being lost. The prevailing Deism insisted on God's existence, but only at the cost of any immediate interaction between God and history. Gordon S. Wood reminds us how difficult it is for us to imagine how great this loss was for the person living at the end of the 18th century. "To conceive of a human world without God's judgments and providences was simply breathtaking; it was in fact what centrally defined the Enlightenment" ("Conspiracy," 414).

What was truly causal in the absence of providence was human contracts and action. Indeed, it can be argued that causes came to be identified with individual motives and wills (see ibid.: 416-20). A major influence here was John Locke. Since innate ideas do not exist (or traditional or cultural influences) the individual is a "blank tablet" on which experience inscribes its content. Thus the cause of evil in the world, Rousseau and others concluded, is institutions corrupting the pure state of nature. If "corrupt and arbitrary power" is removed, human nature is capable of true nobility (see Noll, "Humanistic Values," 118-19).

So for Locke the basis of knowing was experience, but this was defined as human interaction with the natural world, rather than with other people or with God. The true basis of human freedom, Locke said, is economic in the broad sense, rather than social and religious. And Thomas Paine could quote the new French constitution in his *Rights of Man*: "I. Men are born and always continue free and equal in respect of their rights. Civil distinctions, therefore, can only be founded on public utility. II. The end of all political associations is the preservation of the natural and imprescriptible rights of man; and these rights are liberty, property, security, and resistance of oppression" (89).

Notice again that "rights" are defined in economic terms and pertain to the person rather than society. It is not accidental that Adam Smith published his *Wealth of Nations* in 1776. There he defines wealth solely as consumable goods. The general welfare, he concluded, is best served when each person pursues his own self-interest. As with Thomas Paine, freedom is defined as the absence of limitation. What freedom might imply for the treatment of one's neighbor is left for each autonomous individual to decide in his or her pursuit of happiness. The rights of man appear strangely indifferent to the rights of men—to say nothing of the rights of women or minorities, or anyone without property to protect. Consistent with the American preoccupation with its material environment that we surveyed earlier, the primary metaphor for freedom became movement within physical space. Like Leibniz's windowless monads, autonomous individuals, it appears, are destined to realize themselves in constant motion—without real social interaction.

Interestingly, John Locke and Adam Smith were working within a generally Christian framework, so they perhaps would have been surprised at the kind of influence their thinking had. But reflecting on their work, one is forced to agree with Lesslie Newbigin when he writes of this period: "From the point of view of the Bible, the freedom celebrated in the Enlightenment is the freedom offered by the serpent in Eden, the freedom to make one's own decision about what is good" (*Foolishness to the Greeks,* 141). Whereas the Puritan goal was freedom from sin for service to God and one's neighbor, in the Enlightenment it is from arbitrary power, for whatever the individual decided was worth serving.

Though in both cases the individual experience and

expression of that experience is centrally placed, essentially the two are different. For the Puritans, experience was radically subordinated to God's call and purposes; Enlightenment experience becomes autonomous and belief in God is surbordinated to personal rights. G. Groen van Prinsterer was able to see what direction this would take, writing in the 19th century:

> The principle of unbelief—the sovereignty of reason and the sovereignty of the people—must end, while proclaiming liberty, either in radicalism or despotism: in the disintegration of society or in the tyranny of the State, in which all things are levelled without any regard to true liberties and rights. (*Unbelief and Revolution*, 73)

Nineteenth-Century "Perfectionism"

Puritan thinking must certainly be accounted as one of the antecedents of the Enlightenment. "A generation of scholarship," notes Henry May, "has shown us that the main citadels of New England Puritanism were the first to let in the Lockeian infiltrators" (*Ideas, Faiths, and Feelings*, 118). But if the religious character of Puritanism influenced the Enlightenment in America, it was now the secular aspect of that same period that would influence Christianity. If the Revolution had produced an egalitarian state, Christians must now have an egalitarian religion. Nathan Hatch has shown how the major Christian movements spawned during the early 19th century made much of the right of the common person to think for himself or herself. Barton Stone, founder of the "Christian" Church, may be taken as typical. He calls his being cut free from the Presbyterian Church his "declaration of independence" (Hatch, "The Christian Movement," 550). He rejected not merely his denomination, but all traditions and structures, insisting that he needed no creed but the

Bible, no name but Christian. "Everyman for himself, and God for us all!" became his cry (see Woodbridge, Noll, and Hatch, *The Gospel in America,* 163-64).

In one sense, as Hatch points out, this attitude is simply an extension into the church of the revolutionary hatred of privilege and oppressive structures. But in a deeper sense, it is a celebration of the sovereignty of the individual and his or her experience—an application of the rights of man to Christianity. As another Disciples' leader, Alexander Campbell, put it: "Liberty is no where safe in any hands excepting those of the people themselves" (in Hatch, "Christian Movement," 554). In a period in which received certainties were collapsing, it was tempting even for Christians to conclude that all values, rights, and duties resided in the individual.

It is not surprising that the personal expression of the individual came to be formative for religion in the 19th century. Revival hymnody, for example, is in clear continuity with Puritan conversion narrative. These hymns almost exclusively emphasized prayers and testimony over older praise forms. Their purpose, Sandra Sizer believes, was to create a community of intense feelings in which individuals "would thenceforth unite with others in matters of moral decision and social behavior" (*Gospel Hymns and Social Religion,* 52). In revivals during the 1850s, in fact, testimonies actually replaced the sermon. Sizer concludes: "The reduction of all significant knowledge to testimony about the individuals' emotional states made it virtually impossible to gain a wider perspective on the Bible or on theological issues" (137).

Revivalism, of course, has left its mark on all subsequent periods of American history. We have already noted how important this heritage is for our American hopefulness: how intensely revivals focused on Christian experience. Timothy Smith notes how closely linked were the revivals and the perfectionist impulse. The experience of many believers suggested that the struggle with sin could be won and righteousness could be visibly manifested. Notes Smith: "An important by-product of revivalism's triumph over Calvinism was that American theology stood increasingly upon the practical, empirical foundation of Christian experience" (57). The experience of holiness became the key to (especially Methodist) evangelism (137).

The hope for a Christian America was clearly a public one, but its roots lay deep within the experience of the individual Christian. As James Moorhead argues, the apocalyptic vision of history prominent in the 19th century found deep resonance in each individual. The "stress on conversion and sanctification established a complex symbolic linkage between each person's destiny and the millennial sense of history" ("Between Progress and Apocalypse," 538). In the experience of conversion each person was able to know the dramatic intervention of the God of history, which he or she would know more completely at death.

For his part, Henry Thoreau professed not to understand death. He belonged to a group of Americans that put a different color on the American centrality of experience. Their common source was Emerson, who opined in "Self-reliance" that every heart vibrates to the iron string of one's deeper self. In this essay Emerson promotes human experience in ways influential up to the present. On Emerson's view real creativity is identical with spiritual self-reliance. To do original work one must clear a channel down to one's true self. This channel is clogged with cultural debris, religious flotsam and jetsam, and social habits. These must all be cleared away. Mark Twain's famous advice seems to rest on a similar metaphor: "Every now and then take your mind out and stamp on it, to keep it from getting all clogged up."

In a distant and much distorted echo of Thomas Hooker, Emerson urges us to trust ourselves. Each person must realize that "the power which resides in him is new in nature, and none but he knows what that is which he can do, nor does he know until he has tried" (*Essays*, 176).

Thoreau tried to find out on the shores of Walden Pond.

Walt Whitman tried too, as he celebrated himself. Whitman, of whom Thomas Carlyle once said that he supposed he was a big man because he lived in a big country, wrote these lines about mid-century:

> I celebrate myself, and sing myself,
> And what I assume you shall assume,
> For every atom belonging to me as good belongs to you.
>
> I loafe and invite my soul,
> I lean and loafe at my ease observing a spear
>   of summer grass . . .
>
> Creeds and schools in abeyance,
> Retiring back a while sufficed at what they are,
>   but never forgotten.
> I harbor for good or bad, I permit to speak
>   at every hazard,
> Nature without check with original energy.

From "Song of Myself"

Adam became a key symbol of the literature of this period. The American was the new Adam striding across Eden with the innocence and vitality of youth. The individual was a figure of heroic innocence and vast potential. But the drama of this freedom was played out within the dimensions of each person's experience.

In a way similar to their revivalist cousins, these writers implied that the struggles of history were reduced not only to the individual's capacity for experience—in this they shared a common romantic impulse—but they were also collapsed into the present moment. R. W. B. Lewis points out that writers of mid-century focused all their attention on the present.

> The Now was the only portion of *time* important to the writer, because if the immediate could be jostled long enough, beams of the Eternal would begin to show up in it; and it was with the Eternal that poetry had to deal. This

92

was the tactic of writers like Emerson and Thoreau, and occasionally even of Herman Melville: they manipulated the concrete and transient to the point where, in the climaxes of paragraphs, they could set off metaphysical skyrockets. (*The American Adam*, 119)

As with Locke, so here it is the interaction with nature—the concrete and the transient—the economic relation, that defines the human character. The eternal is to be found in our contact with nature—there the real fireworks are set off, rather than with our neighbor or God.

Yet there is a continuity between these celebrations of existence and the Puritan conversion narratives. All problems assumedly can be attacked by the "celebration of the representative self as American, and of the American self as the embodiment of a prophetic universal design" (Bercovitch, *Puritan Origins*, 136), even if now the celebration is no longer a dialogue but a monologue. And it is just this celebration that is most characteristic of our own century.

Client-Centered Counseling

From the bewildering array of movements in our century we focus briefly on that movement in psychology that goes under the name of client-centered counseling and the selfist pop therapies it has influenced.

Around 1920 at Columbia University, John Dewey had established himself as a major cultural influence. His views of education, for example, focused on the individual's interaction with experience in the process of forming fundamental dispositions. His successor William H. Kilpatrick defined education as "the process of continuously remaking experience in such a way as to give it continually a fuller and richer content and at the same time to give the learner ever increasing control over the process" (191). Notice that the goal is to give the student control over the environment, and the means is a fuller and richer content and elaboration of experience. Notice the realm of individual experience is still central, and this experience is still defined over against the environment.

Carl Rogers originally set out to be a minister and enrolled at Union Seminary in New York City. There he fell under the influence of Kilpatrick, and decided that all he wanted to accomplish could better be done in counseling. The goal of his therapy was to give the client an atmosphere of complete acceptance in order to produce a climate of growth. "This acceptance of each fluctuating aspect of this other person makes it for him a relationship of warmth and safety, and the safety of being liked and prized as a person seems a highly important element in a helping relationship" (Rogers, *On Becoming a Person*, 34). This environment then makes it possible for the client to be free and so to cope more adequately with her problems. Notice that freedom, as in the Enlightenment, is made possible by deliverance from an oppressive environment.

Another psychologist from this circle at Columbia is Abraham Maslow. He has become famous for his hierarchy of needs and also for his description of peak experiences. In the latter the real uniqueness of individuals is most pronounced.

> If in many respects, . . . men are interchangeable, then in the peak-experiences, roles drop away and men become least interchangeable. Whatever they are at bottom, whatever the word "unique self" means, they are more that in the peak-experiences. . . . [In these] the individual is most here-now, most free of the past and of the future in various senses, most "all there" in the experience. (*Toward a Psychology of Being*, 108)

Notice the assumption that roles diminish rather than define or extend the self, and that a purely atemporal experience does the most to make one a unique person.

94

Interestingly, Paul Vitz proposes that it may have been major Protestant pulpiteers in New York City—notably Harry Emerson Fosdick and Norman Vincent Peale—who allowed these ideas to pass into common currency in America. In any case, in the last two decades popular self-help therapies and their best-selling manuals have multiplied inside and outside the church.

One of the earliest of these was Thomas Harris's *I'm OK—You're OK*, which focuses on the feelings we harbor in our relationships. The book encourages the reader to develop positive feelings that foster growth. Behavior learned from authority figures that reinforces an image of defeat and failure must be overcome. For, he writes, "the prominent by-product of the frustrating, civilizing process is negative feelings." But there is a bright side: "In the Child is also a vast store of positive data. In the Child reside creativity, curiosity, the desire to explore and know . . . and the recordings of the glorious, pristine feelings of first discoveries" (26, 27). As with Maslow, creativity has nothing to do with parents or society but with innate capabilities of the person.

As in so many professions, these popular views do not represent the best thinking of clinical psychology today. Indeed, one sees among professional counselors a healthy corrective in the growing emphasis on family and contextual therapies. Among the public, however, the selfist views we are examining are still all too common. And variations of these pop theorists appear regularly on best-seller lists.

Perhaps the most familiar form of this thinking is represented by the counter-culture and its New Age children. Theodore Roszak stated his convictions in this way: "I work from the conviction that the growing ethos of self-discovery is charged with all the moral power we find in such high ideals of the past as the rights of man, the assertion of human equality, the belief in worldly progress, the struggle for social justice. The secret of the power is the spontaneous conviction and wonder that self-discovery brings into the life of every human soul it touches" (*Person / Planet*, xxix-xxx). Though Roszak insists on the novelty of this ethos of self-discovery, in many respects he harks back to impulses deep in our history. We must make this project of life our own, experience it deeply and personally, and then find language to describe the depths of our experience.

This last move, of finding a language, we find most difficult. In fact, unlike that of our Puritan ancestors, our stammering may be most symptomatic of our spiritual poverty. As Bellah and his colleagues put it, those interviewed for *Habits of the Heart* are "each in his or her own way confused about how to define for themselves such things as the nature of success, the meaning of freedom, and the requirements of justice. Those difficulties are in an important way created by the limitations in the common tradition of moral discourse they—and we—share" (21).

Conclusion

The polemic against ideas we have been describing, what is called in Christian circles "secular humanism," has come to dominate Christian conversation about American culture. And our survey has uncovered considerable evidence that the roots of American individualism are indeed more secular than Christian.

Our discussion of the significance of these values for communicating and living the gospel, however, must begin with a more general recognition that, whatever the roots, individualism has come to define American culture. Bellah and colleagues conclude: "American cultural traditions define personality, achievement, and the purpose of human life in ways that leave the individual suspended in glorious, but terrifying, isolation. These are limitations of our culture, of the categories and ways of thinking we have inherited, not limitations of individuals . . .who inhabit this culture" (ibid.: 6).

The truth is, much as many of us dislike the excesses to which individualism is prone, we are all socialized to be self-realizing individuals. Robin M. Williams, Jr., for example, concluded his sociological analysis of American society by noting that all American values point to a central constellation: the value of the individual personality. "The ethical, decision-making, unitary social personality is the object of this cult of the individual" (*American Society*, 463).

Moreover, these values are learned very early. Comparative studies on the way Japanese and American babies learn show marked cultural differences within the first few months. Japanese babies seem passive, Americans active. Japanese mothers do more lulling, carrying and rocking, Americans more chatting and talking, as though to stimulate the baby to activity. The researchers concluded: "It is as if the American mother wanted to have a vocal, active baby, and the Japanese mother wanted to have a quiet, contented baby. In terms of the styles of caretaking of the mothers in the two cultures, they seem to get what they apparently want" (Caudill and Weinstein, "Maternal Care," 84).

With its encouragement of human initiative and the individual's (seemingly unlimited) potential for growth and development, this culture encourages personal growth and facilitates entrepreneurial skills. Indeed, in many respects the only measure of goodness is what is good for the individual self. In *After Virtue*, Alasdair MacIntyre has recently described the havoc this has caused in ethical discussion. He notes that, in general, rights language—what is demanded by the individual—has come to replace virtue language—the good practiced by the person—in our conversations about the good.

Emphasis on rights and potential, however, does not help to understand responsibility, let alone limitation and tragedy. The other side of the expectation of success we noted in the last chapter is the promethean tendency of our cultural heritage. There is a widespread and deeply diffused hubris in the air we breathe.

The result is that we treat both other people and society at large as opportunities for our individual growth. A major problem with a preoccupation with my individual development is that it provides no intrinsic value "for you," except as an environment for my growth. Friendship is the arena for pursuit of personal goals. Marriage is seen primarily as a relationship that facilitates my growth (my rights), rather than an opportunity for service and mutuality (my responsibilities). Even the family is commonly seen as a place where persons can develop into self-reliant individuals. In the larger society, competition is one of the primary means of social interaction. Competition provides an environment in which the growth of each individual is encouraged and specific goals achieved. Teamwork ordinarily is understood not as genuine social exchange, but as a group of individuals working toward a common goal.

As a result, personal and highly transient experiences are valued. Christopher Lasch has described this problem in his popular book *The Culture of Narcissism* (1979). There he points out that we have come so to value deeply felt but momentary feelings of well-being that we exploit everything, even relationships, for these feelings. "Americans have not really become more sociable and cooperative, as the theorists of other-direction . . . would like us to believe; they have merely become more adept at exploiting the conventions of interpersonal relations for their own benefit" (66). Goals and a sense of mission must not only be personally espoused but they must actually be created out of personal preference and desires. Charles Garfield discusses this in an amazing study, *Peak Performers* (1987). Peak performers create their own mission by determining what they care about and devoting themselves to that pursuit. Success can be predicted, he argues, when one puts preference before expertise, trusts intuition, and allows personal values to motivate.

The value we place on individual development and achievement deeply influences our view of community. In general, Americans do not join groups for what they can contribute, but for what they can get out of them. People working at volunteer agencies report that the major reason people volunteer their time to help someone else is personal: to feel good about themselves.

Richard Sennett, in fact, has argued that modern Americans have virtually no social sense at all. Space and time have only private and no public meaning. As we saw in our discussion of Maslow, social roles have no positive values; so we see concerted (i.e., social) action as only artificial. Sennett notes that "in modern social life adults must act narcissistically to act in accordance with society's norms. For that reality is so structured that order and stability and reward appear only to the extent that people who work and act within its structures treat social situations as mirrors of the self" (*The Fall of Public Man*, 326-27). This primacy of the personal may be understood by reference to the following diagram (see Sennett; and Mary Douglas, *Natural Symbols*):

Traditional Cultures: Highly structured	American Culture: Low structure
Relationships assumed, roles understood, making public life possible	Personality ascendent, relationships negotiated Public life projection of personal desires
Identity given in context	Identity invented in interaction with the world

Diagram of continuum of individual and corporate understandings of culture.

The primacy of the personal over the social makes it clear why Americans have difficulty developing shared conceptions of corporate structures, such as the city or politics. Christians as well share this more general cultural myopia. I have frequently wondered, for example, how often our distrust of "social action" as a legitimate factor in evangelism is cultural rather than biblical. We do not believe in it partly because we do not really understood what it is.

Communicating the Gospel

It is not hard to conclude that the major single problem for American social life is the problem of relationships—we do not understand them and cannot maintain them. We have seen that one of the historical roots for this problem is the tendency to define ourselves in economic or material terms. We find our meaning more often in our possessions, and the status they confer, than in our relationships. Roy Lichtenstein's cartoon character reproduced at the beginning of this chapter reflects the paradox of America's individualism. On the one hand we are taught to be strong, tough, and self-sufficient—the war hero and tough cop dominate our television programs. But at the same time, we struggle with our relations with others. Is our failure in the latter a consequence of the former?

On the level of communicating the gospel, Christians share many of these tensions, and therefore the pain (and the joy) that they cause. We struggle with our neighbors to maintain a healthy family life and develop meaningful and long-term friendships. This is obviously the level at which any honest communication must begin. If we are going to communicate the gospel in an American context, it will be in the language of personal development. Our technological prowess and our emphasis on human rights, the proliferation and vitality of our Christian institutions—these are all evidence of the value of this tradition. Our failing marriages, our profound loneliness, and our desperate search for ourselves—these are also evidence of this tradition.

Now it is not surprising that so many expressions of the

100

gospel deal with issues of relationship and personal identity. Indeed, it is hard to think of a better way to begin conversations with middle-class Americans. So Robert Schuller, whom we look at in the next chapter, deals with self-esteem; Billy Graham talks about peace with God; and the famous four spiritual laws focus on the broken relationship with God and its consequences. These and many other approaches to evangelism are often criticized as not being fully biblical, which indeed may be the case. But their problems may reflect the limitations of the culture that formed them rather than a specific perversion of biblical truth.

As we have noticed throughout our study, the gospel affirms these personal values at some points, and transcends them at others. The eternal value of the individual and the capacity for personal growth are values Scripture endorses. The many valuable studies of stages of faith and spiritual growth also feature these values. "Self-esteem" and "peace with God" are clearly important handles for Christian understanding.

But there are dimensions of biblical truth these values obscure. One might argue, for example, that God does not mean us to be individuals at all, in our cultural sense of being self-sufficient. Although there was Christian input into the way we speak of individuality, the basic content of autonomous individualism is not biblical. We are not made to be individuals (from the Latin, that which cannot be divided); we are created in and for relationship. This is underlined by our creation in God's image. Images exist only as they reflect and embody that of which they are an image. In the biblical teaching we are made to image the God whose being is fellowship and love among Father, Son, and Holy Spirit. This means that a proper understanding of human life must take seriously our basic rootedness in God and our need to nourish ourselves in his loving character. This is the way we must describe the Good News that Christ died to bring about.

Secondly, the Bible makes it very clear that we exist as human individuals only in community—first in families, in social groupings, and supremely in the family of God. As Paul Vitz notes: "In the religious interpretation the individual and society are not in conflict but in *fundamental cooperation*" (49). In biblical terms we discover who we are by loving, first God and then our neighbor as ourselves. Since God is the covenanting God, we can reflect him by entering covenant relationships that reflect his transcendent purposes.

The fact that all this is difficult for modern people to comprehend reflects a deeper problem: we have no sense of having lost these basic relationships, of being estranged either from God or from each other. We do not even have a language to describe our lostness. We have come to believe that all our drives are basically good, though psychologists point out that "aggression, including destructive aggression, is a natural, intrinsic property of humans, present from birth" (ibid.: 38). We have referred to the conclusions of Bellah and his colleagues that middle-class Americans lack a language with which to articulate their personal preferences. This is because they lack a sense of community, and a narrative sense of their history. We have seen that both of these are casualties of our imperialistic sense of self.

Prophetic Discipleship

Christians are used to lamenting this idolization of human experience. But in a sense we are all implicated in this self-centeredness. As a people we harbor a faith in our essential American innocence and the intrinsic corruption of other people. One has only to recall some of the arguments President Reagan used to support his Star Wars initiative: we can trust American technology. Even in our churches I suppose our emphasis on discovering our gifts is somewhat out of proportion to the importance it is given in the New Testament. Moreover, our emphases on Christian growth and victorious living are a reasonable Christian expression of cultural values. While it is not necessary to say more along these lines, it is pertinent to observe that a great deal of the rhetoric used against secular humanism ignores the many and subtle ways we too reflect these values.

What understanding of community can we derive from our American context? Unfortunately, Christian thinking about community, like that of their secular neighbors, too often assumes the priority and value of the isolated individual, and seeks to understand community in these terms. We start from the individual and move toward relationships. Notice even our vocabulary of friendship speaks of this struggle: we "make" friends, we "work" on our relationships. The Bible understands things differently. There the individual finds his identity in the community. From the very beginning Adam and Eve were created in a covenant relationship with each other, with God, and with the created order. It was obvious that they would only develop their gifts and value in that context. Individualism in our modern sense of self-sufficiency seems more closely related to the attempt of Adam and Eve to be their own gods. The self-realizing, self-defining individual too often becomes a barrier to hearing the cries of his neighbor or obeying the voice of God.

On the one hand, the gifts and value of the person are given by virtue of one's creation in God's image. Therefore, use and development of these gifts glorifies God. On the other hand, because of sin these gifts are invariably used to isolate oneself from God and others—to become independent.

So one might define the "I" that is crucified with Christ as this self-realizing individual. Clearly what must die in the New Testament view is the sense of self-sufficiency, not only with respect to God but also each other. "I have been crucified with Christ; it is no longer I who live, but Christ who lives in me; and the life I now live in the flesh I live by faith in the Son of God, who loved me and gave himself for me" (Gal. 2:20). The conclusion of Paul's teaching in that epistle is that this dying with Christ has freed us to serve one another in love (Gal. 6:2).

So in dying with Christ the believer thinks first of the "we," rather than the "I." Rather than beginning with the individual and seeking to work toward relationship, we begin in community, the body of Christ, and there discover our true identity. The truth is, of course, that we do have individual gifts and identity because we are responsible first to God, and then to our neighbor. But individuality is something that is given to us rather than something invented or achieved. What have we, Paul asks, that we have not received? If we received it, why do we boast as though it were not a gift (1 Cor. 4:7)? Just as we do not know what it means to be whole unless we understand brokenness, so we will not understand individuality unless we are willing to give it up.

So we can encourage our neighbors in their quest to discover themselves by pointing them to Christ. And we can do this quite honestly. For he has promised to give life to all who come and drink of his life-giving Spirit. But we who follow the Lord soon discover that finding ourselves involves an ending, a death. The self that we find given back to us is now in the new relationship Paul describes: we are "in Christ." And being in Christ we are also in his body, the church.

Again, some voices around us in America understand that wholeness must come out of suffering, life out of death. Flannery O'Connor represents the Southern tradition that still has much to teach us about being human. She was once asked why she distorted her characters in such a dramatic way. Her answer was very interesting. For most of her audience, religious values have no meaning. She concluded:

> The novelist with Christian concerns will find in modern life distortions which are repugnant to him, and his prob-

lem will be to make these appear as distortions to an audience which is used to seeing them as natural; and he may well be forced to take ever more violent means to get his vision across to this hostile audience. When you can assume that your audience holds the same beliefs you do, you can relax a little and use more normal means of talking to it; when you have to assume that it does not, then you have to make your vision apparent by shock—to the hard of hearing you shout, and for the almost-blind you draw large and startling figures. (*Mystery and Manners*, 33-34)

Why does O'Connor portray her characters as freaks? Because, she answered, we in the South "are still able to recognize one. To be able to recognize a freak, you have to have some conception of the whole man, and in the South the general conception of man is still, in the main, theological" (ibid.: 44). Perhaps the weakness of our witness has something to do with our loss of the sense of the outrageous and the intractable evil resident in our nature, and the hubris represented in our attempts to "be ourselves." Much of our pride is legitimate, based on our value in God's sight. But as we have observed, often this value is not neutral; it can as easily be enlisted in opposition to God as in service to him.

CHAPTER SIX

Forays into an American Gospel: Walter Rauschenbusch and Robert Schuller

WHETHER THEY LIKE IT OR NOT, AMERICAN CHRISTIANS, WE are arguing, reflect the complex of values we have surveyed. Various ones have of course spoken out against this or that aspect of their culture; others have claimed, often without knowing it, these characteristics as part of the gospel. But in our own century, the growing role of the social sciences has made us more conscious of our American setting. The two cases we examine here represent distinct stages of this consciousness, and thus are important examples of the gospel's interaction with American culture. Walter Rauschenbusch lived during the first generation that studied what was called Christian sociology; Robert Schuller is the heir of a longer tradition, touched on in the last chapter, that made use of psychological principles in preaching and ministry. As a result, the former is much less self-conscious about his use of culture than the latter. Both, however, base their critique of received theological traditions on their reading of cultural trends. And both offer valuable lessons on the use of culture in understanding and proclaiming the gospel.

106

FORAYS INTO AN AMERICAN GOSPEL

Walter Rauschenbusch: Prophet of the Social Gospel

In one sense it is strange to use Rauschenbusch as an example of American theology, since he was raised and ministered for most of his life in the narrow circles of the German Baptist Church. But in very important ways he symbolizes the American desire for a theology that responds to actual life. And his theological reflection quite consciously included the cultural trends he observed around him.

Walter Rauschenbusch was born in 1861, the son of a German pastor and professor in the Rochester Theological Seminary. All his life he carried the burden of his evangelist father to bring men and women to Christ, and sought to become a missionary to India. His testimony after two summers of work in a small rural parish during his seminary years reflects his goals:

> It is no longer my fond hope to be a learned theologian and write big books; I want to be a pastor, powerful with men, preaching to them Christ as the man in whom their affections and energies can find the satisfaction for which mankind is groaning. (In Stackhouse, "Formation of a Prophet," 139)

Though Rauschenbusch had a thorough theological education both in America and in Germany, the decisive influence on his life was the ten years (1887-1897) he spent in the Second German Baptist Church in the blighted "hell's kitchen" area of New York City. During this period he was exposed to the worst effects of the Industrial Revolution. As a pastor he could not ignore the problems of his people and he was pushed to develop a "social theology." This push he later (in 1913) admitted did not come from the church, but from outside.

> It came through personal contact with poverty, and when I saw how men toiled all their life long, hard, toilsome

107

lives, and at the end had almost nothing to show for it; how strong men begged for work and could not get it in hard times; how little children died—oh, the children's funerals! they gripped my heart—that was one of the things I always went away thinking about—why did the children have to die? (In Sharpe, 429)

The problem the young pastor faced was how to combine his evangelical desire to bring people to faith in Christ with his belief that God did not want his people to continue in their wretched situation. As he put it in the same 1913 address, he could not doubt his faith in personal regeneration—("[a person] can be saved by justification. After that, he can be sanctified. Finally, he will die and go to heaven")—but neither could he doubt that the great task of changing the world and making it righteous was important ("Somehow I knew in my soul that that was God's work." See ibid.: 221-22). How do these two things relate? he wondered.

The answer that gradually took shape in his preaching and writing was that only a fresh understanding of the kingdom of God could bridge this gap. This conception he believed was central in Jesus' teaching, and had been lost by the church. The kingdom is the dynamic ideal of establishing a community of righteousness among mankind, the "energy of God realizing itself in human life" (Rauschenbusch, *Theology for the Social Gospel*, 141). It allows scope for both individual and social redemption. Making use of the millennial expectations so prominent in American history, he believed that many factors were converging to suggest that a new great awakening was taking place. God was going to do a great social and religious work in his day, and this could only be understood as the realization of the kingdom.

We will comment on the process of his thinking about God and the Bible below, but here we note ways in which Rauschenbusch used his cultural and historical situation. A dominant theme of his writing and speaking is that the church had lost touch with the modern world. As a result its older methods of personal evangelism no longer worked. They must, Rauschenbusch argued, be replaced by newer methods that appeal to positive social motives (see Sharpe, 395-98). He wrote in his first major work, *Christianity and the Social Crisis* (1907): "The gospel, to have full power over an age, must be the highest expression of the moral and religious truths held by that age. If it lags behind and deals in outgrown conceptions of life and duty, it will lose power over the ablest minds and the young men first, and gradually over all" (339).

Here is a clear example of an awareness that the gospel must be put into terms that the world will understand, even if it does not accept them. But what are these newer social motives that Rauschenbusch insisted were crucial? He started with the belief that "the world is in travail with a higher ideal of justice" (ibid.), that it is moving toward a new era of social righteousness. The gospel must be put into relevant language if it is to be heard in the modern period: the gospel explains and interprets these social hopes.

Some have argued that Rauschenbusch at this point was the heir of the tradition of social reform; others insist he was applying the 18th-century missionary impetus to the problems of the Industrial Revolution; still others believe he was simply expressing the new theology emanating from Ritschl and Schleiermacher in Germany. However important these influences may have been, it is at least arguable that Rauschenbusch is expressing a particularly American desire for a practical salvation. If this is so, his theology can be judged as an early attempt to contextualize the gospel for late 19th-century industrial America. Let us review some evidence for this view.

Rauschenbusch, in the first place, is the heir of American millennial hopes that a new world is about to dawn. In *Christianizing the Social Order* (1912) he enthused: "There is a presentiment abroad in modern thought that humanity is on the verge of a profound change. . . . We feel that all this wonderful liberation of redemptive energy is working out a true and divine order in which our race will rise to a new level of existence" (121). That this is identified with the millennial hope is clear from an earlier chapter of that book, where he soars to even greater heights. A great challenge, he notes, lies before the American churches, and they may fail. "But for the present the East is aflame with the day of Jehovah" (29).

A similar appeal closes his earlier book *Christianity and the Social Crisis*, which recalls the address of Winthrop in its breathtaking scope:

> Perhaps these nineteen centuries of Christian influence have been a long preliminary stage of growth, and now the flower and fruit are almost here. If at this juncture we can rally sufficient religious faith and moral strength to snap the bonds of evil and turn the present unparalleled economic and intellectual resources of humanity to the harmonious development of a true social life, the generations yet unborn will mark this as that great day of the Lord for which the ages waited, and count us blessed for sharing in the apostolate that proclaimed it. (422)

Though, as with the pilgrims, this hope is clearly tied to God's promises to his people, there is just as forceful an application of these hopes to this historical period. Though Rauschenbusch never applied this to America quite as closely as his colleague and friend Josiah Strong, clearly America is the primary arena for this work of God. Here then Rauschenbusch continues a tradition of identifying America with God's redemptive program that reaches back to the beginning of her history.

Secondly, as a result of this, Rauschenbusch feels he can appeal to a vast store of moral enthusiasm among the people he addresses. Even in the book which is written about the "social crisis," his purpose is positively to summon "faith enough to believe that all human life can be filled with divine purpose" (ibid.: 355). Not only is the new order of righteousness possible, but we must all be involved in its realization. Here the moral optimism of the revivalist tradition clearly informs his language.

This is even clearer in his later work *Christianizing the Social Order*, which was written in 1912 to "summon the Christian passion for justice and the Christian powers of love and mercy to do their share in redeeming our social order from its inherent wrongs" (x). He is under no illusion that the task is simple. "The awakening of the churches is far from complete. . . . It will require at least one generation under the most favorable conditions to make this enlargement of the religious conceptions the common property of all" (ibid.: 24). But the hope for a world-forming Christianity, even in the face of the enormous problems he saw around him, continued to drive him on.

Third, this hope centered on the value and resources of the individual personality. True, he had much to say about the harmful aspects of individualism. But from start to finish he called for a conversion of individuals. Only converted men and women were sufficient for this great task because "I believe in the miraculous power of the human personality. A mind set free by God . . . is an incomputable force" (ibid.: 460). His biographer Dores Sharpe, in fact, points out that Rauschenbusch's conception of the kingdom is a merging of his commitment to religious individualism and his concern for social righteousness (*Walter Rauschenbusch*, 220).

So the starting point for Rauschenbusch is the infinite value of the individual. His appeal is for the kingdom of God to come and transform the individual and social lives of people. "Remember," he insisted, "the Kingdom of God can never come perfectly in the world until it comes perfectly in your own life" (in ibid.: 228). Here Rauschenbusch uses the language of Horace Bushnell in his call for personal religion. Social Christianity, he liked to say, encourages personal religion. "It creates a larger life and the power of growth. . . . Live religion brings a sense of emancipation, the exhilaration of spiritual health, a tenderer affection for all living things, widening thoughts and aims, and a sure conviction of the reality and righteousness of God" (*Christianizing*, 113). This is for him both the secret and the goal of the new social order: "It is not this thing or that thing our nation needs, but a new mind and heart" (ibid.: 459).

The vocabulary that Rauschenbusch uses here is often Christian—he calls, for example, for a new apostolate. But the language is American: it is the individual, his or her development, and the individual expression of these hopes that are the religious focus and the social dynamic. Part of the strength of Rauschenbusch's description of Christianity is that though he calls for a new social conception of faith and a new solidarity with the needy among us, he does this in ways that preserve the value of the individual personality.

Fourth, Rauschenbusch sought a practical Christianity that would deal with housing and land use, as well as forgiveness and eternal life. As is evident from his early testimony, Rauschenbusch wanted to influence lives in an immediate way. Personal faith was central and individual transformation was important, as we have seen. But at the same time, Rauschenbusch's evangelical conscience could not rest in the face of the monstrous problems that the Industrial Revolution brought about. Somehow he knew that dealing with these issues "was God's work. Nobody could wrest that from me. Jesus Christ had spoken too plainly to my soul about that. I knew that he was on the side of righteousness, and on the side of his poor brother" (from a 1913 address quoted in Sharpe, 221-22).

Here the initiative of the individual was fused with the practical call of "frontier" life in America, a frontier that had now moved to the slums of America's cities. Henry May, in fact, has argued that the social gospel was a spontaneous response to these growing problems: "In these years of rapid industrialization free men, heirs of the self-reliant tradition of agrarian America, were suddenly finding themselves at the mercy of distant corporation executives. To such men, and to the immigrants who worked by their sides, passive endurance was not acceptable advice. Threatened with un-employment and faced with drastic cuts in already low wages, labor's instinct was to fight" (*Protestant Churches and Industrial America,* 91; and see p. 163 on the rise of social Christianity). Whether or not this is the major cause of social Christianity, clearly Rauschenbusch's response reflects a deep-seated American desire for a faith that worked in the practicalities of life.

The continuing influence of the frontier environment is evident in the centrality of land in Rauschenbusch's thought. In *Christianity and the Social Crisis* he argues that "the owner-ship of the land is the fundamental economic fact in all communities" (14). As he pointedly recalls, the Hebrew prophets concurred that "the social prosperity, the morality, the rise or decline of a people, always fundamentally depend on the wisdom and justice with which the land is distributed and used" (ibid.: 220-21). The freehold myth that communal-ly held and worked land has beneficial effects reappears in Rauschenbusch. "The salutary element in our system was . . . that the land was so evenly distributed among the people and was so accessible to all who were able to use it" (ibid.: 224). Injustice has come about, he argues, because the free land has been used up and so property is not able to play its proper role as a "means of grace" (ibid.: 341-43). These principles must be reapplied in the new urban setting.

Rauschenbusch's Prophetic Discipleship

Having reviewed the ways Rauschenbusch employs charac-teristic American values, we must now ask this: was the Word of God able to provide Rauschenbusch with a critical perspective for understanding these elements? In one sense it certainly did. No one can accuse Rauschenbusch of acquiescing to American values. In the area of land use, for example, though he accepted the value of working and owning land, he radically opposed individual ownership or the idea that economic values were more important than human needs. Two areas in particular illustrate the way the gospel, as Rauschenbusch understood it, provided a critical vantage point for his assessment of his setting: individualism and the drive for material success.

Clearly Rauschenbusch accepted and championed the infinite value of the individual. Yet in his final book, *A Theology for the Social Gospel* (1917), he castigates the individualistic theology that permeated the churches.

> The individualistic gospel has taught us to see the sinfulness of every human heart and has inspired us with faith in the willingness and power of God to save every soul that comes to him. But it has not given us an adequate understanding of the sinfulness of the social order and its share in the sins of all individuals within it. (5)

The kingdom of God, Rauschenbusch believed, enables us to see our witness in the world in terms of social solidarities, rather than to individuals alone. Redemption then can be seen as the progress of society toward a moral order. So while individualism provides a starting point and a moral dynamic, it cannot offer an adequate conception of social reality or of God's work in society. "A realization of the spiritual power and value of these composite personalities must get into theology, otherwise theology will not deal adequately with the problem of sin and redemption" (ibid.: 75-76).

A second area where Rauschenbusch's conception of the gospel provided critical leverage was the call to sacrificial participation in society. Some of his most unforgettable passages reflect a call to let the needs of others determine our economic goals.

An additional vase or rug in a wealthy woman's drawing room may add nothing to the real comfort of any one; yet it may embody the excess toil of a thousand girls for a week. If each girl had been able to retain that additional fragment of earnings, it might have meant an excursion on Saturday, a concert . . . something to give the feel and joy of life. Instead of that it is bottled up in that vase to which a few satiated ladies may say "Ah!" (*Christianizing*, 250)

In a moving passage addressed to college students, Rauschenbusch challenges them to use their gifts and opportunities for Christ rather than for personal advancement. Unlike the culture around him, Rauschenbusch accepts the value of suffering for and with the fallen world. Will we follow Jesus and use our strength on behalf of the poor?

By our opportunities and equipment we rank with the strong. . . . Many of us have inherited social standing and some wealth; it may not be much, but it raises us above the terrible push of immediate need. What relation do we propose to have with the great mass of men and women who were born without the chances which have fallen to us without exertion? Do we propose to serve them or to ride on them? . . . Here is a test for college communities more searching than the physical test of athletics, or the intellectual tests of scholarship. Do we feel our social unity with the people who work for their living, and do we propose to use our special privileges and capacities for their social redemption? (*The Social Principles of Jesus*, 43-44)

Here the prophetic call of Jesus to take up one's cross daily runs against the values of economic advancement that American culture gives us; indeed, it insists that those very values be overturned by Christ's service to the poor.

So our initial reading indicates that Rauschenbusch does use the gospel to provide a critical perspective on culture. But the deeper question our study raises is whether the

Word of God which brings us the gospel has been allowed to be the final authority in assessing cultural currents. In this we must judge that Rauschenbusch fails to allow a genuinely critical theology that preserves the authority of Scripture. This becomes clear when we examine the way Scripture functions in the development of his theology.

We noticed above that the challenge that faced Rauschenbusch during his pastorate in New York was this: how should he combine the personal call to conversion in the New Testament with the obvious call to righteousness that his urban environment suggested? Now this dilemma was typical of that faced by many progressives who were raised in evangelical homes of that time. Unlike many of his contemporaries, however, Rauschenbusch went back to Scripture to determine the answer to his question. There he was led to focus on two areas: the teaching of the Hebrew prophets and that of Jesus, especially his focus on the kingdom of God.

So far so good. Indeed, Rauschenbusch was among the first in our century to understand the central role that the kingdom of God played in Jesus' teaching. But the problem was in the way he came to conceive of the kingdom. On the one hand, Jesus taught that the kingdom involved a moral transformation that would work like leaven or salt in society. But on the other hand, Jesus spoke of the kingdom as a radical break with this present order that would come suddenly in God's time like a thief in the night.

Since Rauschenbusch preferred the first image over the later, he denied that that dramatic imagery was really authentic to Jesus' teaching. Here it is clear that his conception of the kingdom owed as much to 19th-century theology as it did to the New Testament. Following Albrecht Ritschl, Rauschenbusch believed the kingdom was an ethical reality which advances according to the laws of organic growth. The kingdom of God, wrote Rauschenbusch, is the "energy of God realizing itself in human life" . . . "humanity organized according to the will of God . . . the reign of love" (*Theology for the Social Gospel*, 141-43). Here too he reflects the wide-spread cultural impulse for renewal that existed at the end of the 19th century. He saw his era leading to the imminent realization of the kingdom on earth. By his own confession it was the previous commitment to this process, which he already believed was God's work, that led him to settle on the kingdom of God as the key idea.

But what about those elements in Jesus' teaching that speak of the kingdom as a radical break? What of those warnings about the shock and surprise of its coming—as a thief, or with fearful portents in the created order? These apocalyptic elements, Rauchenbusch concluded, were an alien element in which "the sunlight of the prophetic hope gave way to the limelight of the apocalyptic visions of later Judaism" (*Christianity and the Social Crisis*, 35). James Moorhead has pointed out that biblical studies in general at the end of the last century were critical of dramatic interventions into history, seeing them as "an aberration from the main direction of biblical thought" ("The Erosion of Postmillennialism," 63). But the result was that Scripture was not allowed to play a genuinely critical role and biblical teaching on the kingdom was skewed. True, God was seen as working out his purposes in history, but the enlargement of his role in history was bought at the cost of any dramatic intervention to judge or guide that process. Norman Perrin, whose work has been an important element in the recovery of Jesus' actual (and difficult) teaching on the kingdom, concluded of Rauschenbusch's treatment of the kingdom that "it is not an interpretation of the teaching of Jesus at all. It uses a mosaic of ideas drawn together from many different places and then reads these back into such aspects of the teaching of Jesus as can be made to bear them" (*The Kingdom of God*, 47).

The temptation to read Jesus' teaching in terms of the reigning doctrine of progress was encouraged by still another blind spot. Rauchenbusch seemed fundamentally unable to grasp the radical character of human sin and the brokenness

117

this has caused. We have seen that American optimism makes this a particularly common cultural failing, one we will examine in more detail below. He shared the realism of many of his contemporaries in noticing that evil resided in the structures and institutions of the time, but he was not able to relate this to individual sin and responsibility.

Rauschenbusch, for example, could not see that labor unrest reflected any evil in labor, any "badness of men"; it rather reflected a relish for "applied Christianity" (*Christianizing*, 195). A few pages later he does note that a person is responsible for whatever freedom and power he has. But this means that since modern business people have been given more power they have greater responsibility. This is reminiscent of Bruce Kuklick's conclusion that at the end of the 19th century only a very few people were any longer held to be responsible. The progress was a recognition that people exist in networks of relationships (progressive orthodoxy's inheritance from evolutionary thought). But the question that remained was: how is each person to be held accountable? Kuklick notes: "Theologians asked not how every individual was responsible, but how they could be responsible for the many who were not" (*Churchmen and Philosophers*, 227).

So in the end, the authoritative element in this instance is not Scripture, but the historical context in which gathering faith in progress, itself fueled by the revival mentality formed earlier in the century, raised hopes—unrealistically, as it turned out—that a new day was dawning.

The example of Rauschenbusch stands as a clear warning to those who wish theology to respond to the issues of the day. For Scripture has a larger agenda than that provided by our context, and it must finally be allowed to put our concerns in their proper perspective. Rauschenbusch understood and preached the continuity between our work and the work of God—that God does call us to reflect his values in the work we do. But he was not able to see the fundamental failure—

the basic human rebellion against God and his purposes—
that made the death and resurrection of Christ necessary.

But there is another failure which recalls a recurring
weakness in American theology. Rauschenbusch and his
friends represented only one segment of a radically plural-
ized society, and their perspective was severely limited by
their own social location. Robert Handy, a major historian of
the social gospel, has recently written this:

> White Protestants set out to make "still more Christian" a
> civilization which they already assessed highly and in
> which they saw themselves as the best examples and
> guides for the future. . . . A radically pluralized and urban-
> ized society required significantly different and varied
> ways of relating faith to culture. Ironically, the conviction
> that their civilization was so fully democratic and Chris-
> tian that it was almost ready for the kingdom was one of
> the things which prevented them from hearing clearly the
> voices of their fellow black evangelicals, who might have
> helped them to broaden and correct their bright vision. (*A
> Christian America,* 158)

So the weakness of Rauschenbusch and his colleagues
was a common one in American history. Not only did they
fail to hear the voice of God speaking the hard words of
Scripture, but they also excluded minority voices from an
analysis of their situation. Again, the conviction grows that
only a genuine conversation among all members of a society
allows us to properly formulate the pressing questions with
which we confront Scripture. Such humility may also prepare
us to allow Scripture to have the last word.

Robert Schuller's Healing Gospel

As in the case of Rauschenbusch, Robert Schuller's roots are
northern European—typical of much middle-class Chris-

tianity we have assessed. Born on a farm in Iowa in 1926, he was raised in a Dutch Reformed home. This background had a decisive influence on his attitudes. From his mother he learned never to give up, to keep looking up. His dad taught him that "it's almost impossible to be a loser unless you think and accept losing mentally" (in Voskuil, *Mountains into Goldmines*, 8).

In 1943 he began working his way through Hope College and Western Seminary in Holland, Michigan. He liked to recall that he "worked [his] way through college as a janitor cleaning toilets" (in ibid.: 10). And in 1950 he married Arella De Haan and took a church in suburban Chicago.

From the beginning, much as with Rauschenbusch, the motivation for Schuller's work and thinking was evangelistic. The question that burned in his heart was this: "where can I best invest my life to tell others about Jesus Christ" (Schuller, "Hard Questions," 20). So in 1955, when the Reformed Classis of California invited him to form a church in Garden Grove, he eagerly accepted. On the train back from his initial visit, he recalls thinking that the greatest churches in the world have yet to be formed (*Move Ahead with Possibility Thinking*, 7).

Though he began services in a drive-in theatre, he soon was asking Richard Neutra, a leading architect, to design a church building. He had found that the informality and openness of the drive-in setting had created an openness to the gospel, so he wanted a space with a similar openness. Already he understood the importance of a person's cultural and psychological setting.

From Neutra he learned that the natural habitat for people was a garden. He saw that people "were designed to live in gardens. The eyes long to look out upon hills, flowers, and trees; and we should hear songs, water, and birds. This is tranquilizing, and conditions us for creative communication" ("Hard Questions," 14). Perhaps, he concluded, we can use this relaxation for a higher purpose, to lead people back to the

Father-God. "But tension blocks the capacity to hear and to add a new dimension to our consciousness" (ibid). Neutra sought to embody this in the building, completed in 1961.

By the 1970s he had outgrown this building, and he approached Philip Johnson to design an even more spectacular environment for encouraging people to hear the gospel. By the time the Crystal Cathedral was completed in 1980 it had cost almost $20 million and had become one of the most widely discussed structures of our century. To criticisms that such expense represented a wild extravagance, Schuller responded by referring to the medieval cathedrals built to the glory of God.

As with Rauschenbusch, it is possible to trace influences on Schuller back into the last century. There healer and hypnotist P. P. Quinby began a movement that has been called the New Thought Alliance (Mary Baker Eddy was one of Quinby's most famous patients). This in turn had an influence on Russell Conwell, who argued in his famous 1905 sermon "Acres of Diamonds" that it is wrong for a Christian to be poor. All of this was popularized by Norman Vincent Peale, especially in his best-seller *The Power of Positive Thinking* (1952). Interestingly, Peale has often appeared as a guest speaker in Schuller's church and early on endorsed his ministry.

But it is conceivable that Schuller was simply seeking an effective way to communicate the gospel in an American middle-class setting. Like these 19th century precedents, he was simply reflecting deeply held values, and making use of them in communicating his faith. Let us examine more carefully the way this attempt to contextualize the gospel developed.

As already noted, Schuller's overriding concern was to be used of God in bringing people to faith in Christ. He considers himself primarily an evangelist. As he looked around him in Garden Grove, he saw the vast indifference to Christianity. He was greatly distressed that most people, even the clergy, were not concerned about this secularization. He immediately determined that he had to discover "the cultural tempo of the unchurched people" (in Voskuil, 42). So he asked himself: "What human condition exists here that I can have a mission to?" ("Hard Questions," 19). His answer was this: people exist in "the condition of being emotionally hungry" (ibid.). And this answer determined the entire shape of his ministry.

The basic problem with people, Schuller concluded, was their dissatisfaction with themselves and their lives. Now, of course, he admits that people's real problem is that they are sinners and therefore do not have a relationship with God. But people in our culture, he argues, do not *feel* this need. What they do feel is an emotional hunger for personal acceptance and esteem.

This point is so important to Schuller's strategy that we must understand it carefully. Consistent with his basic understanding of human communication and growth, he believes that we should never introduce negative images; indeed, we should never even visualize a negative image or emotion. The reason for this seems to be twofold. First, Schuller points out that people already have an unhealthy supply of negative attitudes and feelings. American culture has conditioned them to believe that they can always do more than they have done. Failure and feelings of inadequacy are always one's own fault. People, accordingly, do not need an additional burden of guilt laid on them in the name of religion. They need deliverance! Secondly, visualizing possibilities mobilizes resources to overcome problems. God has made people in such a way that attitudes have a large influence on what we are able to accomplish. We fail because we choose to fail; we succeed because we believe we can (see Voskuil, 77ff.).

It is at this point that Schuller introduces his famous possibility thinking. Still as a part of his strategy to get the secularist's attention, he points out that there are two kinds of people in the world: those who believe they can succeed and those who believe they will fail. Here is the creed of the possibility thinker:

> When faced with a mountain
> I will never quit
> I will keep on striving
> until I
> climb over,
> find a pass through,
> tunnel underneath,
> or simply stay and
> turn the mountain
> into a gold mine!
> with God's help! (in ibid., 84-85)

In introducing the concept of possibility thinking, Schuller is still operating at the level of communication strategy. He admits that just as feelings of dissatisfaction are not the same thing as awareness of sin, so thinking positively is not the same thing as trusting in God. But speaking of these things will encourage unbelievers to think in the direction of Christian truth. It will provide an atmosphere in which people will be open to listen to the gospel.

And this is what Schuller believes is the primary responsibility of the church. In his most substantial book, *Self-Esteem: The New Reformation* (1982), he seeks to lay out his theology of mission. "As a missionary, I find the hope of respectful contact is based on a 'human-need' approach rather than a theological attack" (12). Moreover, just at this point the church must be reformed. The decline of Christianity in the West, Schuller believes, is the result of placing "theocentric communications" (abstract theology about God) over "the meeting of the deeper emotional and spiritual needs of humanity" (ibid.). The church must take more seriously its calling to reach out to the world; it must in fact die as a church and be reborn as a mission. This is the new reformation.

But what is the theological framework that underlies

123

this strategy and emphasis on mission? Of all the television preachers, perhaps Schuller is the most self-conscious about this. Let us examine this by exploring what Schuller believes to be the true order of salvation.

First, Schuller takes as his starting point that God accepts people. Here his Reformed tradition is evident in what he calls his creation theology. Self-esteem is *"the human hunger for the divine dignity that God intended to be our emotional birthright as children created in his image"* (ibid.: 15). In a recent interview he admits to dissatisfaction with the term "self-esteem," which has been subject to abuse and misunderstanding. But it seems to him the best term he knows to indicate "the state of psychological, emotional and spiritual health Adam and Eve had before the Fall" ("Hard Questions," 15).

Second, this basic calling is reflected in our felt need for esteem and love. "The need for dignity, self-worth, self-respect, and self-esteem is the deepest of all human needs" (*Self-Esteem*, 34). Our fallenness is reflected in the fact that we too often believe that we are nobody. Since we believe that we are nobody, we believe we cannot do the right thing. "I don't think I am," Schuller notes, leads to "I don't think I can."

All of this reflects a more basic problem: we are sinners. Here too Schuller seeks to make the connection with current widespread feelings of inadequacy. Sin for Schuller is the inability to trust oneself, others, and, most importantly, God. True, Adam rebelled against God, but the original sin that resulted was "a terribly weak and insecure ego" (in Voskuil, 101). It is true, moreover, that we continue to rebel against God, but this merely hides our basic negative self-image. Guilt consequently is "the negative emotion experienced by a 'conscience-mind' that passes a personal moral judgment upon itself" (in ibid., 105).

As we will note presently, just at this point Schuller appears most vulnerable to criticism. Is Schuller expressing the traditional doctrine of sin in a modern vocabulary, or really redefining it in modern terms? On the one hand, his terms are obviously carefully chosen to make his point in the modern context. Speaking of dissatisfaction with oneself is a way of reminding people of their sinful situation, without insulting them (ibid.: 73). Sin must never be presented in a way that merely reinforces a negative self-image. On the other hand, Schuller is well aware that people must be brought to the point of seeing their need of God as the only means of restoring self-image. This implies what in traditional terms is called repentance. Even this is not self-abuse, however, but rather a positive creative force. It is, Schuller reminds us, a *metanoia*, a change of mind. It implies a recognition that God's love and acceptance overcome our own insecurity.

Schuller's call to commitment illustrates his view of the substitutionary atonement behind our salvation. Here is the prayer he asks people to pray:

> Jesus Christ, I accept You as my forgiving Savior. I don't understand what Your death on the cross means. But I know that in some way You died for me. I remember the old Jewish prophet who spoke about You when he said, "He was wounded for our transgressions, he was bruised with our iniquities, the chastisement of our sins was upon his shoulders." I remember an Indian chief who once said, "Fire cannot burn where fire has already burned." You have by Your suffering and death on the cross accepted the responsibility of my sins. You have fulfilled the justice that demands that wrong be punished. And you mercifully promise to extend this forgiving credit to my account. By Your death justice and mercy are both fulfilled. Thank You, Jesus Christ. Amen. (In Voskuil, 108)

Notice in particular two aspects of this prayer of confession. First, Schuller clearly believes in the importance of the substitutionary death of Christ. Christ suffered and died in place of the sinner so that she can be restored to a right relationship with God. This is entirely by God's grace and cannot be earned or deserved. But notice secondly, although it is not made explicit here, this redemptive event is tied to the problem of self-esteem. The hell that Christ experienced for the sinner was the total loss of self-esteem and separation from God. Moreover, the end that is achieved in the sinner is the restoration of that esteem. God in Christ declares us to be righteous and thus frees us to love ourselves. Schuller summarizes:

> I see self-esteem as the sense of value that comes to me when I have been restored to a relationship with God as the heavenly Father, and I have the assurance that I am worth a lot. Christ has died on the cross for me. If he thinks that much of me, I had better start thinking something good about myself. ("Hard Questions," 20)

Schuller is often accused of limiting Christian experience to peace of mind, but this misses the final step that he believes necessary for the believer. Self-esteem, whatever its weaknesses as a theological category, is not the end of faith, according to Schuller. The end is rather being equipped to serve God and his creation in the world. Godly self-esteem does not encourage self-indulgence, but self-denial in service to God. The observer of Schuller's ministry might be excused for thinking the goal of Christian discipleship is worldly success. But in fairness to Schuller, this is not his intent. Success, in fact, is carefully defined as "building self-esteem in yourself and others through sacrificial service to God and your fellow human beings" (in Voskuil, 140). Characteristically, Schuller reminds us that self-denial is not self-debasement! Only the person with a healthy self-esteem is prepared to serve God and her neighbor.

Schuller's Contextualized Message

Any evaluation of Schuller's ministry must begin with the recognition that his innovations grow out of his mission. It is

Schuller's attempt to communicate the gospel to a complacent audience that leads him to reformulate the message. This is no excuse for any resulting distortion, but rather an important starting point for understanding what he is doing.

As we have noted throughout our study, since the time of the New Testament the most lively and creative reflection on the gospel has taken place in a missionary setting. Indeed, one might even argue that this is the setting in which God intended his people to think through their faith in every era. One need not agree completely with Schuller's dictum—that the church must die as a church in order to be reborn as a mission—to see that placing evangelism closer to the center of our life would help us see the gospel more clearly. Indeed, in dialogues between Schuller and theologians one has the feeling the two sides are not speaking the same language and are therefore talking past each other. As Schuller himself laments: "Some time ago I was speaking with some theologians whose beliefs were faultless. But they had no consciousness of how their theology touched the daily thought and emotional systems of real people. They simply were not touching the hurts of people" ("Hard Questions," 19). For this sensitivity Schuller is to be applauded.

How can we evaluate Schuller, however, not only in his method but in his understanding of Scripture and the gospel? Let us begin first with Schuller's communication of the gospel to his culture. Here he certainly has touched one of the deepest felt needs of American middle-class culture. There is in fact a growing body of evidence that a clear correlation exists between self-esteem and social problems. In California, a state-wide task force, appointed by the governor, is studying this particular issue. Its assignment is to study the relation between a lack of self-esteem and social issues and then to suggest ways that society and government can improve people's self-esteem.

Across the country, meanwhile, book stores continue to expand their self-help sections.

The common criticism made against Schuller, that he "focuses too intently upon the self" (Voskuil, 146), is therefore misplaced. Schuller, it might be argued, is simply reflecting the preoccupation of his culture with personal and emotional issues. There may well be a problem here; our society may be obsessed with these issues to excess, but the fact is that this is our world and the gospel must be put in its terms. Communication of the gospel must deal with the demands of the self. If there is a problem here, it may be the problem of American middle-class culture, rather than Schuller's way of communicating the gospel.

Christ's death may well need to be expressed as his experiencing a loss of self-esteem and his total humiliation for us; sin may have to be described on one level as a basic inability to trust oneself. These expressions are a part of the communication of the message of God's love. The Sunday morning services in which these terms are used, Schuller is careful to explain, are not meant to be explanations of biblical teaching; they are evangelistic forays into the unbelieving world. The Crystal Cathedral has in fact, by any standard, one of the largest and most sophisticated programs of lay training in the world. A director of that program (with a Ph.D. in theology) told me in conversation that traditional orthodox views and the breadth of biblical interpretation are fully explored in these classes. All of this proceeds with Schuller's full cooperation.

So Schuller is attempting to speak of Christianity in a language that his audience will hear. Particularly, he wants to communicate that what they perceive as their major problems, low self-esteem and emotional loneliness, can only be addressed through commitment to Christ. So far so good. But now we must ask the second question: does Scripture provide a critical perspective by which self-esteem may be evaluated and understood? Does it nourish a discipleship that critiques and corrects that cultural context in which it is carried out?

Here it appears that Schuller has allowed his cultural context not only to provide the terms for communicating the gospel, but also a framework in which the gospel is finally understood. Martin Marty, writing in the preface of *Self-Esteem: The New Reformation*, asks, "Is not this a philosophy which makes room for God more than a theology that incorporates philosophy?" (11-12). Schuller responds by reminding us that as an evangelist he finds that the human need approach provides a more "respectful contact" than the theological attack (ibid.: 12). This may be true, but the fact remains that human needs must find their content and meaning in some larger perspective of human life and history than their immediate cultural and psychological context.

The fact is that Schuller is nowhere able to subject the "positive thinking" approach to any fundamental critique. It is not enough to disclaim responsibility by insisting that he is a psychologist who is also a theologian. True, Schuller does insist that commitment has a pricetag of self-denying service. But the final emphasis on positive and creative thinking can easily become a procrustean bed on which experience must be made to lie. Listen, for example, to what advice he gives those who live in the ghetto and face its challenges. "If you live in a community where racial prejudice does, in fact, exist, . . . don't use this as an excuse to keep from trying. Use it as a challenge to hurdle over the obstacle" (in Voskuil, 78). One might argue that it is just this attitude, characteristic of the white middle class, that has reinforced long-intrenched and structural injustice.

This illustrates the fact that possibility thinking is simply "an inadequate perspective from which to view life" (Voskuil, 155). It encourages a deep-seated American tendency to evade and ignore negative aspects of life, aspects that cannot be addressed in a fallen world without suffering, defeat, and sometimes even death.

A further weakness is that sin is defined as primarily a lack of self-esteem and only secondarily rebellion against

God. (Schuller believes it is one of the weaknesses of historical theology that this order has been reversed.) As Voskuil points out, one might argue that we have too much rather than too little self-esteem. Indeed, placing the emphasis on my lack of self-esteem takes away responsibility for my actions. I am responsible for rebellion against God and his instruction; I am not responsible for my lack of self-esteem. Self-esteem then may well be an essential instrument to open a hearing for the gospel, but when a commitment is made, this concept must be subjected to severe biblical scrutiny.

Discussion of the Christian life in America will characteristically include references to emotional failure and personal feelings of inadequacy. But these discussions must be reformed in the light of Scripture. Emotional pain will be the expression of a basic rebellion and inability to listen to God's word; inadequacy will only be properly recognized when we see ourselves as the prodigal son who has consciously fled from the father's house. In assessing Robert Schuller's contribution to an American theology, we can be grateful for the bold way in which the gospel is put into contemporary categories. But we can also point out that the gospel's freedom has been finally impaired when these categories become normative. One has the feeling that in the work of Schuller American middle-class culture has not been critically reformed.

CHAPTER SEVEN

Conclusion

CULTURE IS PARTLY A CONVERSATION AMONG MEMBERS OF a society about what is important. We have surveyed some of those topics of conversation for American Christians, and spoken briefly about some responses to those issues. This conversation would sound very different if it were carried on by members of the Indian tribe that John Muir visited. But it should be clear by now that it is not only Americans that have trouble comprehending elements of the gospel. This tribe would have had its own difficulties.

In the Philippines, for example, where we lived and worked, the more personal and communal demands of the gospel were often grasped immediately. Biblical teaching on loyalty, fellowship, and hospitality was understood and eagerly if imperfectly applied. It was my impression, however, that my students there had something to learn from the more abstract and individualistic modes of thinking I knew. The biblical teaching on the covenant, for example, is something more than the personal or family alliance that Filipinos sometimes understood. It is also the promise of God that had timeless and transcendent dimensions. While I could learn from them the importance of personal values, they could profit from the ability to conceptualize ideas in a more abstract (impersonal) way.

It should be clear, then, that what I am saying is not meant as a particular attack on what Americans have done with Christianity. It rather is a special example of the more general problem of human beings hearing and shaping a message that comes from God. If there is validity in our argument, presumably a biblical response to the particular issues that concern Americans would constitute an effective contextualized witness and provide the starting point for a theology that is truly American. It is not our purpose either to elaborate the biblical response or begin the constructive theological work. (Though Robert K. Johnston makes a start in his article on the atonement in an American context, "Acculturation or Inculturation.") But we may outline in this concluding section some of the lines such a discussion might take. What reflection is appropriate to the American middle-class setting we have examined? Let us return briefly to the three complexes of values of American culture: our pragmatism, our optimism, and our humanism.

The Virgin Land Is Not Pure

The value Americans place on their environment seems sometimes to be inversely correlated to their sense of place. While outside the South or New England we are generally a rootless people, we are extraordinarily concerned with resources, either their preservation or their exploitation. Indeed, we saw that in many respects American identity is established in material terms. We define ourselves by our relation to our material environment, perhaps more than our relation to other people (or even to God).

That this has resulted in great material prosperity and

great technical accomplishment we can readily acknowledge. But we noted a dark side as well: Americans invariably tend to endow material means with ultimate or final value. Owning a home, for example, is seen as one of the ends of life rather than a means to other ends. Meaning is attached to accumulating an estate far beyond any conceivable use. These attitudes are as true of the backpacking Californian with her favorite wilderness area as of the business person with his portfolio of investments.

Communicating the gospel in America will invariably reflect these emphases. On the one hand, it will tend to affirm the quest for achievement. It might emphasize that God loves us and seeks to help us realize our potential or our gifts (He "has a wonderful plan for our life"). On the other hand, it will encourage a practical no-nonsense kind of faith, a "faith that works." As we will note presently, it will in general affirm the goodness and value of the person and the created order. As a rule, Christians in America will feel the need of affirmation rather than of deliverance.

But when it comes to living out the Christian faith, American Christians need to take the next step and develop a lifestyle that uses and yet transforms this pragmatism.

For though the world has real value, it is not our final home, nor the locus of final value. Moreover, it has been marred by human sin. The tragic dimensions of our huge appetite for material satisfaction are consistently missing in the American imagination and its literature. A perfect contrast is provided by the attitudes of Australians toward their own Outback. Their frontier, unlike ours, was never conquered. Indeed, its vast darkness conquered them, giving them a sobering sense of human possibility in a fallen world. In what may be the Australian national epic, Patrick White's *Voss*, a German explorer Voss sets out on a major expedition to the Outback. In one encounter after another, the natives, the weather, and the vast distances prove too much for the explorer's party. Finally Voss, lying feverish and near death in his tent, hears that the horses are gone. He says: "We must catch the horses, or we will rot as we lie in this one place."

> As if to rot were avoidable. By moving. But it was not. "We rot by living," he sighed.
>
> Grace lay only in the varying speeds at which the process of decomposition took place, and lovely colours of putrescence that some souls were allowed to wear. For, in the end, everything was of flesh, the soul elliptical in shape. (*Voss*, 382)

Such language sounds abominable to our middle-class ears. For Americans, the land is always a source of hope, and we find ourselves, or escape our past (is it the same?) by moving across it. We do not see the brokenness, the vanity of things that possess us, and so we do not see there reflected our own brokenness. We live with the illusion that rot is avoidable by moving. Forever confusing movement with progress, we are always moving, displaying a kind of Brownian movement of the soul.

At the same time, American reflection on God's Word will focus constructively on the goodness and value of God's material creation. A major theme of American theology, developed recently by Max Stackhouse, is stewardship. In a day of dwindling resources and widespread scarcity of basic necessities, issues of stewardship are urgent. In the world-wide conversation about God's purposes today, Americans can contribute a great deal to discussions about the care and development of creation.

The Dream Does Not Belong to Us

When the Puritans dreamed of founding a city where God would be properly praised, the echoes of hope that centuries of God's people had known were clear (How long, Lord?). But there was one crucial sense in which their project broke with the Christian story. They believed New England was a new and final form of God's work in history. Here they shared the millennialism of the Anglo-Saxon people in general. But their project, they were sure, bode well of being the final stage in God's great program. They would have approved of Herman Melville's characterization:

> Escaped from the house of bondage, Israel of old did not follow after the ways of the Egyptians. To her was given an express dispensation; to her were given new things under the sun. And we Americans are the peculiar, chosen people—the Israel of our time; we bear the ark of the liberties of the world. Seventy years ago we escaped from thrall; and, besides our first birth-right—embracing one continent of earth—God has given to us, for a future inheritance, the broad domains of the political pagans. . . . God has predestinated, mankind expects, great things from our race; and great things we feel in our souls. The rest of the nations must soon be in our rear. We are the pioneers of the world; the advance-guard, sent on through the wilderness of untried things, to break a new path in the New World that is ours. In our youth is our strength; in our inexperience, our wisdom. (*White-Jacket*, chap. 36, 150-51)

But in this Americans only share the fundamental error of God's people in the Old Testament. God's call does not come to people for their sake, but for the world's. Israel was not a city on a hill, but a light to the nations. The dream that burned in the hearts of these first Americans was not for them alone in any special sense, but was a trust given to them for the whole world. The new world is not ours, but Christ's. Therefore the beginning in New England was not a break, but an extension of this great story of God's dream into all the earth.

Whatever its source, however, Americans have come to believe that the good life is their right. Therefore, initially the gospel must come to them like this: God wants to do some-

135

thing new and exciting in our lives. Whatever our past mistakes, God wants to start over with us and make us new creatures. These, of course, are important biblical themes, but they are particularly appealing in an American context. The constructive contribution of America may lie along these lines: that God is good and in Christ has intervened to bring about a new kingdom of righteousness.

But biblical faith in America must ultimately move beyond this emphasis on crisis and beginnings to a sense of connection with the past, and with the world. For the emphasis on newness, on finality, however biblical the language as it came to be used in America, was ultimately defective. It clearly prepared the way for Emerson's fatal division of the party of hope from the party of memory. How tragic that a people who bore and embodied the great story of God's love for the world should do so much to cut out their own story from the larger whole.

It's an irony that we share with the Soviet Union the myth that our societies represent the end of history. I have often wondered how often the real problem behind our mutual suspicion is the shared belief that our particular form of government is the final and universal human society. America has not been able to get away from the belief that the final period is flowering; Russia has not escaped this belief either, having inherited it from Marx's perversion of the Christian view of history. When our negotiators face each other across the table, it is hard for them to relinquish these cherished illusions.

Minority voices in our culture, however, would remind us that there cannot properly be hope for the future without a past. "Without a past," writes John Peale Bishop on the South and tradition, "we are living not in the present, but in a vague and rather unsatisfactory future" (in Woodward, *Burden*, 36). Ironically, because we are bearers of this burden of a new world, we have lost our sense of connection. We are an abstracted people. As Henderson says in Saul Bellow's novel: "Nobody truly occupies a station in life any more. There are mostly people who feel that they occupy the place that belongs to another by rights. There are displaced persons everywhere" (*Henderson the Rain King*, 32).

Robert Bellah and his colleagues insist that Americans can only escape their isolation by regaining a sense of connection with their past. This means reconnecting our American story with the larger story of God's purposes for the world. For there is one unnoticed casualty in our stubborn and forward-looking optimism. Without a memory, we lose our sense of sin. To become aware of one's past is to take responsibility for its mistakes. To ignore our past is not only to doom ourselves to relive it, as Santayana put it, but as we will argue, to make repentance and the entrance of God's grace less likely. For in the concluding lines of (Southern writer!) Robert Penn Warren's *All the King's Men:* "Out of history into history . . . the awful responsibility of Time."

The American Adam Is Fallen

The story of the self is very much the story of American culture. Strangely, the shocks of two world wars and a worldwide depression could not shake our confidence in the limitless potential of human development. One could well say of our century what R. W. B. Lewis says of the 19th century, "What these [people] had to confront was not only the current Adamic dismissal of sin and history but also the cheerful religious air which accompanied the act of dismissal" (*The American Adam*, 175). We will doubt anything except the benign and glorious potential of the self.

Is this partly why we are unable to escape the isolation in which our culture places the individual? The second great need, according to *Habits of the Heart*, is a sense of community. For ultimately some things the individual cannot do alone. Unlike the Indian tribe in Alaska, we have no sense of the

137

absolute limits in which we live. So we cannot properly appreciate community values where the interests of the group take precedence over those of the individual, and when the group can do things for me that I cannot do for myself.

What is wrong for Americans always relates to frustration of desire or frustrated potential, never something that cannot be fixed. God, when he exists, helps those who help themselves. So we cannot conceive of Christ except as a model or moral example. As a result we cannot understand the biblical notion of covenant relationships, which embrace and suffer evil rather than overcome or ignore it. For Americans evil is only a hurdle to leap over, and not an intractable dimension of the fallen order that we must learn to tolerate. So while we move incessantly and we "develop" ourselves without stop, we cannot grow up, either as individuals or as a nation. We are in the end a nation of adolescents.

Not surprisingly, as we have seen, the gospel is often presented in America in terms of "finding oneself" and discovering "real peace" in the midst of our busyness. But for the Christian seeking to follow and grow in Christ, faith should entail a growing sense of inadequacy and of the need for grace. One sure sign of maturity is being able to take responsiblity for mistakes, confessing weakness and inability. This the Bible insists is an essential part of "coming to ourselves" and returning to the waiting father (Luke 15).

A Return to God and to Ourselves

What do we make of this sketch for our Christian witness and discipleship? We will want to discuss separately the implications for our witness and our discipleship. But before we do this, two issues call for extended comment. All our discussions have revolved around two questions that we must now face: American understandings of history and of sin. On the one hand, our incurable optimism has replaced history with anticipation; and on the other hand, Americans have great difficulty understanding sin as rebellion against God, indeed as anything other than a temporary impediment. Discussion of these issues will prepare us to propose a method of communicating the gospel that begins where these problems converge: interpersonal relationships.

Middle-class Americans seem to have lost all sense of a narrative connection with the past. We noticed that our sense of national mission, something which should have nourished a sense of history, of a larger story, has instead been the means of eliminating a sense of the past. This is a serious loss. As Lesslie Newbigin reminds us:

> All understanding of past events is part of one's under-standing of the present and the future. . . . The way we understand the past is a function of our whole way of meeting the present and the future. The community of faith celebrates the resurrection of Jesus as the ground of assurance that the present and the future are not under the control of blind forces but are open to unlimited possibili-ties of new life. (*Foolishness to the Greeks*, 63)

The way Americans deal with the past is a function of our approach to life. Fundamentally, we have two ways of dealing with it: we idealize it or, when this is impossible, we forget it. In our remembering of history we tend to make it an image of what we would like our present to be. The American Revolution becomes an unvarnished struggle against tyranny; the Civil War is the fight to preserve equality; and world wars are noble efforts to make the world safe for democracy. There is just enough truth in these asser-tions to make them plausible, but not enough to preserve us from hypocrisy.

When we cannot idealize, we forget. We like to remember our Civil Rights Movement, but cannot remember all the broken promises that preceded (and followed!) it. As Allan Bloom notes wryly, "Forgetting, in a variety of subtle forms, is one of our primary modes of problem-solving" (230).

A graphic example of this is provided by the ritual means we associate with sickness and death. The rituals of our hospitals and mortuaries are all designed to obscure the unpleasantness of mortality. In our funerals the body is either made up to look natural or is missing altogether, having been conveniently eliminated. A most common expression of comfort is: "Don't worry, everything will be all right." In other words, our rituals are designed to make us forget.

In many cultures however, rituals serve as continual reminders of the dark side of reality. Family members prepare the body for burial, carry it to the cemetery, and assist in the burial. Death anniversaries are remembered with elaborate ceremonies that underline connections between generations. Christianity, when it enters these cultures, serves to encourage believers to face these hard realities and find meaning in them. In the Indian tribe we met in the opening pages of Chapter 2, Christ's death actually underlined the painful realities of war and death that they knew about. It allowed them to see even these in the light of a larger story in which God was active.

Meanwhile, the way we have endowed our present with only a future meaning leads us to focus on those aspects of Christianity which underline newness and future hope. Life in Christ is a new life, unconnected with the past; the world awaits the return of Christ in which everything will be made new. But a central ritual of our faith, the Communion service, forces us to recall the past: as Jesus said, thinking of his death, "Do this in remembrance of me" (Luke 22:19). And in forcing us to remember, it encourages a sense of limits and responsibility. But this leads us to our second problem: Americans have trouble understanding sin.

At first glance this might seem an unremarkable observation. What people does have a proper sense of sin? Although this is a typical American response, truly American culture is uniquely deaf regarding sin. C. Vann Woodward says America's peculiarity

> arises out of the American legend of success and victory, a legend that is not shared by any other people of the civilized world. The collective will of this country has simply never known what it means to be confronted by complete frustration. (*Burden*, 168)

Australia, we noted, has its sober sense of limits; Europe has its existentialism and nihilism. Moreover, there is hardly a Third World country without its elaborate system of sacrifices and ways of appeasing the gods and spirits. A sense of sin, however expressed, would seem to be an almost universal aspect of humanity's creation in the image of God. Whatever we make of the fact, the truth is that we are made for God and there is, as Augustine put it, an incurable restlessness to life apart from God. Religion is the universal attempt to find this way back to God.

America, of course, did not always lack this sense of sin. For many, Puritanism is synonymous with a bad conscience. But in the 19th century something happened to our corporate imagination. Nourished on the confidence of Emerson and Whitman, and by the prevailing evolutionary worldview, by the end of the century the party of hope had triumphed everywhere.

This had a great deal to do with a general loss of individual responsibility, Bruce Kuklick has argued. Progressive orthodoxy, influenced by evolution and German Idealism, pictured our lives as part and expressive of historical processes. But who is responsible then for the problems industrialization has brought us? No one, or at least a very few people who control structures. The rest of us are generally victims of (oppressive) structures and processes. This became a condition not only for losing a sense of sin, but for the demise of the tradition of New England theology. "New

England Theology vanished in America," writes Kuklick, "when what its adherents conceived of as a personal responsibility for depravity came to be regarded as an unhelpful way to think about the social causation of untoward behavior" (*Churchmen and Philosophers*, 229).

Our study has made clear that it is precisely the Christian heritage that has given American culture its dynamic and its optimism. But what we have made of this heritage—hope without sin—has now become a fundamental obstacle to a proper hearing of the gospel. Here the characterization of H. Richard Niebuhr can hardly be improved upon. In *The Kingdom of God in America* he argued that the kingdom of God has been institutionalized and secularized in the American self-image.

> For the golden harps of the saints it substituted radios, for angelic wings concrete highways and high-powered cars, and heavenly rest was now called leisure. But it was all the same old pattern; only the symbols had changed. (196)

At this point Americans most intensely resist the gospel. Not only have they harbored the illusion that they can develop their innate potential for good, but they also invariably have had the resources to pursue this illusion. Individuals can always manage another seminar or another vacation. The major tragedy of our foreign policy has resulted from a combination of our confidence in our "divine" calling and the almost unlimited means to pursue that vocation. If we perish, Reinhold Niebuhr said, the strength of our enemy would only be a secondary cause. "The primary cause would be that the strength of a giant nation was directed by eyes too blind to see all the hazards of the struggle; and the blindness would be induced not by some accident of nature or history but by hatred and vainglory" (*The Irony of American History*, 174).

Even Christians have been influenced by this sense of happy ending. For it has become fashionable to pretend that all our problems either do not exist or can easily be solved by attendance at one more seminar or being more earnest in prayer. Of course, it would be unwise to belittle the good that study can do, or to pretend that there is not a serious shortage of prayer in our churches. What concerns me is this attitude: Christianity is equated with innocence, rather than with struggle and pain. It certainly was not that way in the New Testament, and, at this moment, is not that way in 80 percent of the world.

A Theological and Evangelistic Method for Americans

We return now to the steps of interaction with our culture that we laid out at the beginning of our study. We are ready to ask how the values we have discussed translate into involvement with our neighbors. We will do this in terms of four stages of interaction: from basic communion to transformation (see p. 23).

1. *Shared Stresses / Hopes.* We return to the basic assumption we have made throughout our study that no way exists to begin communicating the gospel apart from beginning with common cultural forms. Missionaries know this intuitively, but we sometimes think this particular rule is suspended in a Christian nation. But this study has made clear that not only do we inevitably share these struggles with our non-Christian neighbors, but that God takes these struggles seriously.

Communication takes place from the known to the unknown. If God came all the way down into our situation to redeem us from sin, can we do any less than share the actual pressures and joys of our community? To love our neighbor is to take this dimension of life seriously.

This will mean in the first place affirming the positive values of American culture: its dynamic, its hopefulness, even its valuing of the individual. The first word in communicating the gospel in America may well be an emphasis on God's affirming love of the individual. True, we often believe the future is bright for the wrong reasons; God promises a future that is filled with promise because of his purposes for creation and his presence in the resurrection of Jesus from the dead. What is wrong is not hope—Christians are not cynics—but misplaced hopes.

Secondly, however, we will have to point out the limitation of these values. Americans do have needs, just as they do have a history, even if their legends serve to obscure both. But it is important to recognize that these needs are the reverse of their cultural strengths. In their dynamic and creativity, Americans hurry by their history; with their individualism and initiative they do not take the time to develop and enjoy relationships.

For all of these reasons it is clear that our greatest weakness is social. We are people who cannot manage relationships, who often cannot even understand the social dimension of life. So Americans typically suffer a great deal over broken relationships, inside and outside the home. Husbands and wives are estranged from each other; parents are estranged and anguishing over children; workers struggle with colleagues and employers. Numerous studies (and our own personal experience) indicate that a large percentage of the people we deal with each day are suffering from some severe, potentially debilitating emotional pain. Here I am often reminded of Sadhu Sundar Singh's comment after visiting Christians in the West (largely in California!): he had never seen such spiritual poverty in all his life in India. Clearly this must be the primary arena in which the gospel must be proclaimed in America.

Moreover, the pain of relationship failure is not something that we can miraculously escape by accepting Christ; rather it is sometimes exacerbated by conversion. This failure we inevitably share with our non-Christian friends, and we will sooner earn their hearing and respect when we admit to our own struggles.

144

Of course other important issues arise in our culture. We may struggle with our neighbors to uphold the integrity and value of our physical environment or of our workplace. Witness begins, in other words, with affirming the value as well as the fallenness of the created order that we share with everyone. This sharing, which rests on our common image of God and the preserving grace of God, is the fundamental means of our communion and communication with those outside of Christ. As it is the fundamental way in which our natural relationships are formed, so it will naturally be the basic means of our communication with them.

2. *Signs of Transcendence.* But what do we make of failure in relationship? Or how do we account for the exquisite joy that this part of our lives can provide? Is there a larger story into which these episodes fit? Is there a larger meaning for the created order that transcends the depletion of resources?

Sooner or later in our exchange we will stumble on elements that cannot be accounted for by this world alone. I say stumble because it is often in very sudden or accidental ways that ultimate questions arise—the sudden death of a loved one, the loss of a job, a child's birth, or an unexpected breakthrough at work. It might as easily be our surprise as that of our non-Christian friend, and it is as important how we deal with this as with our friend. What do we make of this turn of events?

What implications do we draw from the dominant feeling that things are going to turn out all right? We must surely deal with this in our communication of the gospel. How do we respond to this cultural optimism? One response is to insist that people must know that they are sinners before they can believe in salvation. Radio pastor J. Vernon McGee in a recent mailing took this tack in a not-so-hidden reference to Robert Schuller and selfist therapies. "The gospel has nothing to do with your highest potential or your self-esteem. It has to do with your *sins.* Jesus did say that he came not to call the righteous (there were none righteous) but sinners to repentance. He came to seek and to save the lost" (mailing to supporters, August 1986).

From one point of view, McGee is correct. Christ's message did come to sinners. "For I have not come to call the righteous," he said, "but sinners" (Matt. 9:13). McGee is right in what he affirms, but not in what he denies. The gospel does indeed have something to do with self-esteem. Schuller's view is that problems of self-esteem are the vehicle to understanding our need of God and our sin; McGee insists that only an awareness of sin will allow us to make any headway at all in proper self-worth.

Here I believe both the principles of communication and biblical truth teach us that, in this respect, Schuller is correct. Awareness of sin is a result and not a precondition of an encounter with God's love in Jesus Christ. Jacques Ellul makes this point well:

> The basic notion of sin, as found in some preaching and in Calvinism, is that it encompasses everything, and that only when one has the terrible conviction that one is a sinner, does one learn the startling news that one can also be saved. I believe, however, that the Biblical Revelation is exactly the opposite. . . . What the Bible announces is not sin, but salvation. It is only when people learn they are loved, forgiven, and saved—it is only then that they learn they were sinners. In other words, we can take sin seriously only by looking at Jesus Christ on the cross, because it is there that we learn the significance of sin. But it is by learning I am saved that I learn the importance of my sin. Consequently, this too is a message of liberation and absolutely not a message of gloom and condemnation for the human race. (*Perspectives on Our Age*, 104)

We cannot insist a proper understanding of sin is prerequisite to hearing the gospel. What we do explore is the sense of limits, of failure in a given culture. In a fallen world God has ordained that our weaknesses and handicaps can become metaphors of our dependence—on others, on the world around, and ultimately on him. This is why Jesus said that the rich can hardly enter the kingdom of God—they have gotten into the habit of thinking they are self-sufficient. For those with acknowledged needs, there is already a sense of dependence which is an echo of faith. Until people understand their fundamental dependence, they will know nothing about biblical faith. The faith they do have will more closely resemble presumption.

In this we all learn from those in need, just as we learn best from our own trials. Remember that the teaching of the parable of the Good Samaritan (Luke 10:29ff.) is that only the victim can answer that urgent question: who is my neighbor? For only the victim is put in the place where he can recognize redemption when he sees it.

Paul makes this point in Romans 5:6 and 8. There he notes that it was precisely while we were in the state of powerlessness, or inability, that Christ died for us. A sense of inability is not the same thing as a sense of sin, but it is often the means by which we turn from ourselves to God who promises to save us. This leads us then to our third level.

3. *The Challenge of the Gospel.* There comes a day in which we must make it clear that these hopes and frustrations make sense only in the light of what God has done for us in Jesus Christ. The news that on the cross God was in Christ reconciling the world to himself must be seen as the key to the larger story. For in that event God was both taking the suffering of our rebellion and failure on himself, and (in the resurrection) affirming the value and purposes of the created order and giving hope to these values.

Now the question with which we began this study again becomes urgent: what in our culture provides an analogy that can make redemption plausible? We have faced the fact that, at first glance, the main currents of the American middle-class culture converge to make this event appear improbable and unnecessary. This is the point at which, as on Mars hill, those who are listening to us are likely to laugh.

Do we simply continue to proclaim our message and trust the Holy Spirit to bring results? Is this all we can do? I believe not. We have often noted one area in which we consistently feel our failures: interpersonal relationships. All around us are casualties of our optimism who suffer severe emotional injury, betrayal, or disappointment. We often ourselves feel the tensions of strained or broken relationships. As we become sensitive to these needs, they may become for all of us metaphors of our great need for the grace of God, and the means by which we will understand something more of that central transaction between humanity and God on the cross.

Here are materials for discovering the point in our culture which may provide an understanding of Christ's death on the cross. Underlying our surface optimism, there is an abyss of emotional hunger and suffering in our culture. True, Holden Caulfield ended up watching his sister going around on the merry-go-round, looking so nice. But only hours earlier he confessed: "That's the whole trouble. You can't ever find a place that's nice and peaceful, because there isn't any. You may think there is, but once you get there, when you're not looking, somebody'll sneak up and write 'Fuck you' right under your nose" (*The Catcher in the Rye*, 184). We are an estranged and ultimately lonely people.

It may be that this is the way the central message of the gospel will be best understood. The New Testament says that God took our estrangement upon himself. Christ himself suffered the ultimate loneliness to bring down the barriers that keep us separated from each other and from God.

Bruce Kenrick, in his powerful portrayal of middle-class seminarians trying to communicate the gospel in East Harlem, notes how this reality struck them:

> "Think of Jesus hanging on the Cross," a young addict's mother said to a Parish congregation. "Remember how he

shouted out, 'My God, why have you forsaken me?' Well, that's understood by the addict. . . ." This mother understood the cry as well, for she had suffered with her son. Ray's pastor and his lay church friends also understood the cry, for they were suffering with him. They were suffering because "participation in East Harlem's life" meant that Ray Johnson was not "a case," nor an object to be pitied, but a friend to whom they *belonged*, with whose life their lives were interwoven. (*Come out the Wilderness*, 182)

The first word of the gospel in America may be summed up in Christ's words: "Come to me, all who labor and are heavy laden, and I will give you rest" (Matt. 11:28). But in coming to Christ and experiencing his love, there will surely be a growing awareness of the cost to God of the peace and joy that he offers, and that we so deeply yearn for. Seeing the cost will prepare us for the next step: obedience. Here Christ will ask us to take his yoke upon us and learn from him.

4. *Obedience.* When we have heard this news, what are its special implications for us as Americans? As the experience of these seminarians shows, it is only as we move out of our insularity and listen to other voices, not least the voice of God's Word, that we will have the resources necesssary both to witness and to obey responsibly. Obedience for us will involve movement in the direction of real involvement, a reconnection with each other and with God.

Let us reflect further on this point by a look at our fundamental optimism. This attitude raises a central question: Is life supposed to be good, or is it supposed to be difficult? How one answers this question will have far-reaching implications for understanding life and religion. The answer, moreover, is culturally conditioned. In our Indian tribe in Alaska, for example, suffering and warfare were so common that they were assumed to be normal. Life was supposed to be hard. The gospel, when it came, was much more likely to embrace war and killing; indeed, as we saw, it employed these as metaphors for redemption. On the level of communication

149

at least, pain is embraced, good is seen to come out of evil, and following Christ would involve finding meaning in this struggle to survive.

As people of this culture began to live out their discipleship, however, the gospel would begin to work a deep reconciliation among them, and, no doubt, between them and creation. They would begin to see God as sustainer and perfecter of community and creation, and they would begin to question some of their received notions about "normal" life and suffering.

For Americans the answer to our question is very different. We are socialized to believe that life is supposed to be good. We are likely to respond like Christians of Peter's day when confronted with the promise of God's judgment. "Where is the promise of his coming? For ever since the fathers fell asleep, all things have continued as they were from the beginning of creation" (2 Pet. 3:4). Like Holden Caulfield, we believe life is fun, creation is good, and so evil does not seem real. So on the level of communication we will emphasize the love and goodness of God. Though even here, just as the Indian tribe wanted peace, so we fear the loss of love and God's goodness. The light of the gospel will finally show our illusions for what they are, and, as we saw, the cross will illumine sufferings that are really there. Our suffering in relationship will make us long for the wholeness that is only found in Christ.

But when we begin to follow Christ in discipleship, the gospel will cause us to challenge many of these received notions. We will come to see how central suffering and death have to be in a fallen world. God's holiness and justice will come to play the more prominent role they have in Scripture. As the gospel delivered the Indians from bondage to never-ending warfare, so that same gospel will deliver Americans from the no less debilitating illusion that everything will be all right. The one begins with enmity and hears the challenge of Christ's death as reconciliation; the other begins with individual fulfillment and hears the gospel as a fellowship of suffering. Notice that the process of maturity will be different for each, though both come to a deeper insight into reconciliation. For us maturity involves seeing that depth and intimacy in relationship are not possible without sacrifice and suffering.

Our study of American culture has led to the conclusion that American experience puts us in a position to understand and celebrate the goodness of creation and the tradition of wisdom. What is good about our optimism and can-do spirit is that the world can be known and developed because God made it that way. In coming to know our environment carefully and thoughtfully, we will learn something about the wisdom that God has placed there. But by the same token we do not feel the need for deliverance and so find it very hard to understand the prophetic/apocalyptic tradition of Scripture, especially as this came to focus on the cross. We are repulsed by this and find it uncongenial to our mode of thinking. A baby in a manger, Jesus as faithful friend and model—these fit our temperament better than a naked and bleeding man on a cross.

How do we begin to repair this shortsightedness? Certainly one way, we have implied, is by a deeper sympathy with a broken world just outside our suburban neighborhoods, or even the broken lives within that neighborhood. In the light of these cries we might be able to hear the Good News of a crucified savior. Indeed, is it possible in the end to be liberated from our smug security and optimism, to be truly mature in Christ, without exposure to and significant interaction with the minority voices in our culture?

That we are on the right track in these brief comments is made clear by a phrase of Paul's. We may well say of our responsibility to our American culture what he said of his call to the Corinthians. After an opening discussion of the nature of wisdom and human judgments (chapter one), he writes, "I decided to know nothing among you except Jesus Christ and him crucified" (1 Cor. 2:2).

Understanding our creation-based confidence in the world in the light of the cross may lead us to see that we must relinquish some of our privileges. As John Coleman puts it, this may be the only way of salvaging the freedom Americans so desperately desire, and allowing us to celebrate self-giving and self-criticism rather than self-aggrandizement (*An American Strategic Theology*, 286).

What might be some concrete steps that Christians can take to begin the process of self-criticism we are advocating? We conclude by noting three steps of such a process:

1. *Self-awareness.* Much of what we have spoken about in this book is called social analysis by social scientists. The premise of our study is that we must be far more self-conscious about the forces that shape us as Americans. This means that in our churches and fellowship groups we need to have more regular and sustained reflection about the values that actually do shape our behavior (not those we think shape us). A recent study of religious values in Australia discovered that, much to the surprise of everyone, actual religious values played no greater role in the thinking of Christians than they did in the thinking of non-Christians. I often wonder what a similar study would show in our own setting. In any case, the process of growth as Christian Americans must begin and continue with more serious reflection on forces that shape our thinking and acting.

This process of reflection must involve more time for reflection and prayer, both in our corporate and individual lives. We are often busy doing good, but we do not pray; we are effective, but not often reflective. No spiritual growth will take place apart from what we have called "coming to ourselves."

2. *Rereading of Scripture.* Becoming more alert about our cultural values will allow us to approach the text with more honesty. We will be able to ask what Scripture has to say to us in our particular situation. Much of what liberation theologians are saying may not appeal to American evangeli-

cals, but one thing we can learn from them is to reread Scripture in the light of the realities of our situation. A corollary of this is to develop suspicion toward "what we have always known about the Bible." Perhaps what we have always known reflects more eloquently our cultural values than the Word of God. Maturity at least means holding out the possibility that God will say something new to us as we diligently reread familiar texts.

So beginning with the challenges and questions of our lives, we will seek a fresh interaction with the truth of Scripture. God will certainly show us things we had overlooked or forgotten.

3. *Study and Action Groups.* Wherever Christians are serious about their witness and discipleship, they must include an analysis of their situation in their mission strategies. In the local church this might mean forming study and action groups of those engaged in similar work: a group of business people or medical professionals reflecting on their working environment and the possibilities of Christian witness there. This would provide opportunity for the exchange of experience and the development of more serious strategies for Christian impact on our society. If all of this is combined with a more careful study of Scripture and much prayer, we may begin to see a more incarnational ministry in our churches.

Reflection on this process—guided by Scripture and in the light of our Christian traditions (the interaction of Christians at other times with their world)—will in the end prove to be a theological method that will move us ahead. This of course is a big work, for the whole church and for the whole of our lives. But it starts with each Christian who will take his own setting seriously, live in it and love it, as God himself has done in Christ.

BIBLIOGRAPHY

Adams, James T. *The Epic of America*. Boston: Little, Brown, 1931.

Ahlstrom, Sydney E. *A Religious History of the American People*. New Haven: Yale University Press, 1972.

Angell, Roger. *The Summer Game*. New York: Viking, 1972.

Augustine of Hippo. *Confessions*. New York: Washington Square, 1951.

Bavinck, Herman. *Our Reasonable Faith*. Grand Rapids: Eerdmans, 1956.

Bellah, Robert. *Beyond Belief: Essays on Religion in a Post-Traditional World*. New York: Harper, 1979.

—————. *The Broken Covenant: Civil Religion in Time of Trial*. New York: Crossroad/Seabury, 1975.

Bellah, Robert, Richard Madsen, William M. Sullivan, Ann Swidler, and Steven M. Tipton. *Habits of the Heart: Individualism and Commitment in American Life*. Berkeley: University of California Press, 1985.

Bellow, Saul. *Henderson the Rain King*. Greenwich, CT: Fawcett Crest, 1958.

Bercovitch, Sacvan. *The American Jeremiad*. Madison: University of Wisconsin Press, 1978.

—————. *The Puritan Origins of the American Self*. New Haven: Yale University Press, 1975.

BIBLIOGRAPHY

Berger, Peter. *Rumor of Angels: Modern Society and the Rediscovery of the Supernatural.* New York: Doubleday, 1969.

———. "A Sociological View of the Secularization of Theology," in *Journal for the Scientific Study of Religion,* 6 (1967): 3-16.

Berger, Peter, Brigitte Berger, and Hansfried Kellner. *The Homeless Mind: Modernization and Consciousness.* New York: Penguin, 1973.

Bernstein, Richard. *John Dewey.* New York: Washington Square, 1966.

Bloom, Allan. *The Closing of the American Mind: How Higher Education Has Failed Democracy and Impoverished the Souls of Today's Students.* New York: Simon and Schuster, 1987.

Bonhoeffer, Dietrich. *The Cost of Discipleship.* Rev. edition. New York: Macmillan, 1959.

Caldwell, Patricia. *The Puritan Conversion Narrative: The Beginnings of American Expression.* Cambridge: Cambridge University Press, 1983.

Caudill, D. W., and H. Weinstein. "Maternal Care and Infant Behavior in Japan and America," in *Readings in Child Behavior and Development.* Ed. C. S. Lavatelli and F. Stendler. 3rd edition. New York: Harcourt Brace Jovanovich, 1972.

Clebsch, William A. *From Sacred to Profane America: The Role of Religion in American History.* Decatur, GA: Scholars Press, 1968.

Coleman, John. *An American Strategic Theology.* New York: Paulist, 1982.

Commager, Henry Steele. *The American Mind.* New Haven: Yale University Press, 1950.

Conn, Harvie M. *Eternal Word and Changing Worlds: Theology, Anthropology, and Mission in Trialogue.* Grand Rapids: Zondervan, 1984.

Crunden, Robert M. *Ministers of Reform: The Progressives' Achievement in American Civilization, 1889-1920.* New York: Basic Books, 1982.

Davis, David Brion. "The Emergence of Immediatism in British and American Anti-Slavery Thought," in Mulder and Wilson, *Religion in American History.* q.v.

Dewey, John. *A Common Faith.* New Haven: Yale University Press, 1934.

———. *Reconstruction in Philosophy.* Boston: Beacon, 1957.

Douglas, Mary. *Natural Symbols.* New York: Penguin, 1970.

Douglas, Mary, and Steven Tipton, eds. *Religion and America: Spiritual Life in a Secular Age.* Boston: Beacon, 1982.

Dyrness, William. *Christian Apologetics in a World Community.* Downers Grove: InterVarsity Press, 1983.

———. "The Contribution of Theological Studies to the Christian Liberal Arts," in *Making Higher Education Christian.* Ed. Joel Carpenter and Kenneth Shipps. Grand Rapids: Eerdmans, 1987.

———. "How Does the Bible Function in the Christian Life?" in *The Use of the Bible in Theology: Evangelical Options.* Atlanta: John Knox Press, 1985.

———. *Let the Earth Rejoice: A Biblical Theology of Holistic Mission.* Westchester, IL: Crossway Books, 1983.

Edwards, Jonathan. *Basic Writings.* New York: Signet Classic, 1966.

Eliade, Mircea. *Myths, Dreams and Mysteries.* London: Collins, 1957.

Ellul, Jacques. *The Ethics of Freedom.* Grand Rapids: Eerdmans, 1976.

———. *Perspectives on Our Age: Jacques Ellul Speaks on His Life and Work.* Ed. William H. Vanderburg. Trans. Joachim Neugroschel. New York: Seabury Press, 1981.

———. *The Subversion of Christianity.* Grand Rapids: Eerdmans, 1986.

Emerson, Ralph Waldo. *Selected Essays.* New York: Penguin, 1982.

Farley, Edward. *Theologia: The Fragmentation and Unity of Theological Education.* Philadelphia: Fortress Press, 1982.

Feeley, Kathleen. *The Voice of the Peacock.* New Brunswick: Rutgers University, 1972.

Fischer, Kathleen R. *The Inner Rainbow: The Imagination in Christian Life.* New York: Paulist Press, 1983.

Flexner, James Thomas. *Washington: The Indispensable Man.* New York: New American Library, 1984.

Fox, Richard. *Reinhold Niebuhr: A Biography.* New York: Harper & Row, 1985.

Franklin, Benjamin. *The Autobiography of Benjamin Franklin.* Ed. L. W. Labaree, R. L. Ketcham, H. C. Boatfield, and H. H. Fineman. New Haven: Yale University Press, 1964.

BIBLIOGRAPHY

Furnas, J. C. *The Americans: A Social History of the United States: 1587-1914.* New York: Putnam, 1969.

Galbraith, John Kenneth. *The New Industrial State.* Boston: Houghton Mifflin, 1967.

Garfield, Charles. *Peak Performers: The New Heroes of American Business.* New York: Avon, 1987.

Gill, Robin. *The Social Context of Theology.* London: Mowbrays, 1975.

Glazer, Nathan, and Daniel P. Moynihan. *Beyond the Melting Pot: The Negroes, Puerto Ricans, Jews, Italians, and Irish of New York City.* Boston: MIT, 1970.

Goodman, Paul and Percival. *Communitas: Means of Livelihood and Ways of Life.* New York: Vintage, 1960.

Goudzwaard, Bob. *Capitalism and Progress.* Grand Rapids: Eerdmans, 1979.

Groen Van Prinsterer, G. *Unbelief and Revolution.* Amsterdam: The Groen van Prinsterer Fund, 1975.

Guinness, Os. *The Gravedigger File: Papers on the Subversion of the Modern Church.* Downers Grove: InterVarsity Press, 1983.

Hamilton, Edith. *Mythology.* Boston: Little Brown, 1948.

Handy, Robert T. *A Christian America: Protestant Hopes and Historical Realities.* Cambridge: Oxford University Press, 1984.

Harris, Thomas A. *I'm OK—You're OK.* New York: Harper & Row, 1969.

Hatch, Nathan O. "The Christian Movement and the Demand for a Theology of the People," in *Journal of American History,* 67, 3 (Dec. 1980): 545-67.

————. *The Sacred Cause of Liberty: Republican Thought and the Millennium in Revolutionary New England.* New Haven: Yale University Press, 1977.

Hawthorne, Nathaniel. *The House of Seven Gables.* New York: New American Library, 1961.

Heimert, Alan. "The Great Awakening as Watershed," in Mulder and Wilson, *Religion in American History.* q.v.

Hunt, David, and E. McMahon. *Seduction of Christianity: Spiritual Discernment in the Last Days.* Eugene, OR: Harvest House, 1985.

James, Henry. *The American.* New York: Dell Publishing, 1960.

James, William. *"Pragmatism" and "The Meaning of Truth."* Cambridge: Harvard University Press, 1978.

Johnston, Robert K. "Acculturation or Inculturation: A Contemporary Theology of the Atonement," in *Amicus Dei: Essays on Faith and Friendship.* Ed. Philip J. Anderson. Chicago: Covenant Publications, 1988.

Kenrick, Bruce. *Come out the Wilderness: The Story of East Harlem Protestant Parish.* New York: Harper, 1962.

Kilpatrick, William H. *Foundations of Method: Informal Talks on Teaching.* New York: Macmillan, 1926.

Kluckhohn, Clyde. *Mirror for Man.* New York: McGraw-Hill, 1949.

Kozol, Jonathan. *Illiterate America.* New York: Anchor / Doubleday, 1985.

Kraft, Charles H. *Communication Theory for Christian Witness.* Nashville: Abingdon, 1983.

Kuklick, Bruce. *Churchmen and Philosophers: From Jonathan Edwards to John Dewey.* New Haven: Yale University Press, 1985.

Lasch, Christopher. *The Culture of Narcissism: American Life in an Age of Diminishing Expectations.* New York: W. W. Norton, 1979.

Lavatelli, C. S., and F. Stendler, eds. *Readings in Child Behavior and Development.* New York: Harcourt Brace Jovanovich, 1972.

Lewis, R. W. B. *The American Adam: Innocence, Tragedy and Tradition in the Nineteenth Century.* Chicago: University of Chicago Press, 1955.

Locke, John. *Second Treatise on Civil Government.* Ed. Lester DeKoster. Grand Rapids: Eerdmans, 1978.

Lovelace, Richard F. *The American Pietism of Cotton Mather: Origins of American Evangelicalism.* Grand Rapids: Eerdmans, 1979.

Lundin, Roger, and Mark A. Noll. *Voices from the Heart: Four Centuries of American Piety.* Grand Rapids: Eerdmans, 1987.

Lyon, David. *The Steeple's Shadow: On the Myths and Realities of Secularization.* London: SPCK, 1985.

Mabee, Charles. *Reimagining America: A Theological Critique of the American Mythos and Biblical Hermeneutics.* Macon, GA: Mercer University Press, 1985.

MacIntyre, Alasdair. *After Virtue: A Study in Moral Theory.* 2nd edition. Notre Dame: University of Notre Dame Press, 1984.

Maclear, James F. "The Republic and the Millennium," in Mulder and Wilson, *Religion in American History.* q.v.

Malina, Bruce J. *Christian Origins and Cultural Anthropology.* Atlanta: John Knox Press, 1986.

————. *The New Testament World: Insights from Cultural Anthropology.* Atlanta: John Knox Press, 1981.

Marsden, George M. *The Evangelical Mind and the New School Presbyterian Experience: A Case Study of Thought and Theology in Nineteenth Century America.* New Haven: Yale University Press, 1970.

————. *Fundamentalism and American Culture: The Shaping of Twentieth Century Evangelicalism: 1870-1925.* Cambridge: Oxford University Press, 1980.

————. "Perry Miller's Rehabilitation of the Puritans: A Critique," in *Church History,* 39 (1970): 99-105.

Marsden, George M., ed. *Evangelicalism and Modern America.* Grand Rapids: Eerdmans, 1984.

Maslow, Abraham H. *Toward a Psychology of Being.* 2nd edition. New York: D. Van Nostrand, 1968.

Mather, Cotton. *Magnalia Christi Americana: Or the Ecclesiastical History of New-England.* Ed. R. J. Cunningham. New York: Frederick Ungar, 1971.

Mathisen, Robert R. "Evangelicals and the Age of Reform, 1870-1930: An Assessment," in *Fides et Historia,* 16 (Spring/Summer 1984): 74-85.

May, Henry F. *The Enlightenment in America.* Cambridge: Oxford University Press, 1976.

————. *Ideas, Faiths, and Feelings: Essays on American Intellectual and Religious History 1952-1982.* Cambridge: Oxford University Press, 1983.

————. *Protestant Churches and Industrial America.* New York: Harper, 1949.

McClendon, James William. *Systematic Theology: Ethics.* Nashville: Abingdon Press, 1986.

McCullagh, James C. "Symbolism and the Religious Aesthetic: Flannery O'Connor's *Wise Blood,*" in *Flannery O'Connor Bulletin,* 2 (1973): 43-58.

Mead, Sidney E. *The Lively Experiment: The Shaping of Christianity in America*. New York: Harper & Row, 1963.

Melbin, Murray. *Night as Frontier: Colonizing the World after Dark*. New York: Free Press, 1987.

Melville, Herman. *White-Jacket*. Evanston and Chicago: Northwestern University Press and Newberry Library, 1970.

Meredith, Howard L. *The Native American Factor*. New York: Seabury Press, 1973.

Míguez Bonino, José. *Toward a Christian Political Ethics*. Philadelphia: Fortress, 1983.

Miller, Perry. *Errand into the Wilderness*. New York: Harper, 1956.

————. "From Covenant to Revival," in Mulder and Wilson, *Religion in American History*. q.v.

————. *The Life of the Mind in America from the Revolution to the Civil War*. San Diego: Harcourt, Brace and World, 1965.

Miller, Perry, ed. *The Transcendentalists: An Anthology*. Cambridge: Harvard University Press, 1950.

Moorhead, James H. "Between Progress and Apocalypse: A Reassessment of Millenialism in American Religious Thought, 1800-1880," in *Journal of American History*, 71, 3 (Dec. 1984): 524-42.

————. "Charles Finney and the Modernization of America," in *Journal of Presbyterian History*, 62 (1984): 95-111.

————. "The Erosion of Postmillennialism in American Religious Thought, 1865-1925," in *Church History*, 53, 1 (March 1984): 61-77.

Morey-Gaines, Ann-Janine. *Apples and Ashes: Culture, Metaphor, and Morality in the American Dream*. Decatur: Scholars Press, 1982.

Morison, Samuel Eliot. *The Oxford History of the American People*. Cambridge: Oxford University Press, 1965.

Mouw, Richard J. *When the Kings Come Marching In: Isaiah and the New Jerusalem*. Grand Rapids: Eerdmans, 1983.

Muir, John. *Travels in Alaska*. Boston: Houghton Mifflin, 1979.

Mulder, John M., and John F. Wilson, eds. *Religion in American History: Interpretive Essays*. Englewood Cliffs, NJ: Prentice-Hall, 1978.

Nash, Roderick. *Wilderness and the American Mind*. New Haven: Yale University Press, 1967.

BIBLIOGRAPHY

Newbigin, Lesslie. *Foolishness to the Greeks: The Gospel and Western Culture*. Grand Rapids: Eerdmans, 1986.

Niebuhr, H. Richard. *Christ and Culture*. New York: Harper & Row, 1951.

———. *The Kingdom of God in America*. New York: Harper, 1937.

Niebuhr, Reinhold. *The Irony of American History*. New York: Charles Scribner's Sons, 1952.

———. *Moral Man and Immoral Society*. New York: Charles Scribner's Sons, 1932.

Noll, Mark. *The Bible in America*. Cambridge: Oxford University Press, 1982.

———. "Humanistic Values in 18th Century America: A Bicentennial Review," in *Christian Scholar's Review*, 6 (1976): 114-26.

———. *One Nation Under God? Christian Faith and Political Action in America*. San Francisco: Harper & Row, 1988.

Noll, Mark, Nathan Hatch, and George Marsden. *The Search for Christian America*. Westchester, IL: Crossway Books, 1983.

Oates, Stephen B. *Let the Trumpet Sound: The Life of Martin Luther King, Jr.* New York: Harper & Row, 1982.

O'Connor, Flannery. *Mystery and Manners*. Ed. Sally and Robert Fitzgerald. New York: Farrar, Straus & Giroux, 1969.

Paine, Thomas. *Rights of Man*. New York: Willey Book Company, 1942.

Peale, Norman Vincent. *The Power of Positive Thinking*. New York: Prentice-Hall, 1952.

Peirce, Charles S. *The Essential Writings*. Ed. Edward C. Moore. New York: Harper & Row, 1972.

Perrin, Norman. *The Kingdom of God in the Teaching of Jesus*. Philadelphia: Westminster, 1963.

Peterson, Jim. *Evangelism for our Generation: The Practical Way to Make Evangelism Your Lifestyle*. Colorado Springs: NavPress, 1985.

Petersen, William, Michael Novak, and Philip Gleason. *Concepts of Ethnicity*. Cambridge: Belknap/Harvard, 1982.

Potter, David M. *People of Plenty: Economic Abundance and the American Character*. Chicago: University of Chicago Press, 1954.

Preston, John. *The New Covenant or the Saints Portion*. London, 1629.

Raboteau, Albert J. *Slave Religion: The "Invisible Institution" in the Antebellum South.* Cambridge: Oxford University Press, 1978.

Rauschenbusch, Walter. *Christianity and the Social Crisis.* New York: Macmillan, 1907.

————. *Christianizing the Social Order.* New York: Macmillan, 1912.

————. *The Social Principles of Jesus.* New York: Association Press, 1916.

————. *A Theology for the Social Gospel.* New York: Abingdon, 1945.

Rogers, Carl R. *On Becoming a Person: A Therapist's View of Psychotherapy.* Boston: Houghton Mifflin, 1961.

Rose, Anne C. *Transcendentalism as a Social Movement: 1830-1850.* New Haven: Yale University Press, 1981.

Roszak, Theodore. *Person / Planet: The Creative Disintegration of Industrial Society.* New York: Doubleday / Anchor, 1978.

Salinger, J. D. *The Catcher in the Rye.* New York: New American Library, 1953.

Schaffer, Francis. *The Christian Manifesto.* Westchester, IL: Crossway, 1978.

Schneider, Herbert. *A History of American Philosophy.* 2nd edition. New York: Columbia University Press, 1968.

————. *The Puritan Mind.* Ann Arbor: University of Michigan Press, 1958.

Schuller, Robert. "Hard Questions for Robert Schuller About Sin and Self-esteem," in *Christianity Today,* August 10, 1984, pp. 14-24.

————. *Move Ahead with Possibility Thinking.* Introduction by Norman Vincent Peale. New York: Doubleday, 1967.

————. *Self-Esteem: The New Reformation.* Waco: Word Books, 1982.

Segundo, Juan Luis. *Our Idea of God.* New York: Orbis, 1974.

Sennett, Richard. *The Fall of Public Man: On the Social Psychology of Capitalism.* New York: Random, 1978.

Sharpe, Dores R. *Walter Rauschenbusch.* New York: Macmillan, 1942.

Shelley, Bruce. *Evangelicalism in America.* Grand Rapids: Eerdmans, 1967.

BIBLIOGRAPHY

Sizer, Sandra S. *Gospel Hymns and Social Religion: The Rhetoric of Nineteenth-Century Revivalism.* Philadelphia: Temple University Press, 1978.

Smith, Henry Nash. *Virgin Land: American West as Symbol and Myth.* 2nd edition. Cambridge: Harvard University Press, 1970.

Smith, James Ward, and A. Leland Jamison, eds. *The Shaping of American Religion.* Princeton: Princeton University Press, 1961.

Smith, Page, ed. *Religious Origins of the American Revolution.* Decatur: Scholars Press, 1976.

Smith, Timothy L. *Revivalism and Social Reform in Mid-Nineteenth-Century America.* New York: Abingdon, 1957.

————. "Righteousness and Hope: Christian Holiness and the Millenial Vision in America, 1800-1900," in *American Quarterly,* 31 (Spring 1979): 21-45.

Stackhouse, Max L. "The Formation of a Prophet: Reflections on the Early Life of Walter Rauschenbusch," in *Andover Newton Quarterly,* 4, 3 (1969): 137-59.

————. *Public Theology and Political Economy.* Grand Rapids: Eerdmans, 1987.

Strong, Josiah. *Our Country.* New York: American Home Missionary Society, 1885.

Sweet, William Warren. *The Story of Religion in America.* New York: Harper, 1950.

Taylor, Charles. *Philosophy and the Human Sciences.* Cambridge: Cambridge University Press, 1985.

Thoreau, Henry David. *Walden.* New York: Modern Library, 1950.

Tocqueville, Alexis de. *Democracy in America* (2 volumes). New York: Vintage, 1945.

Turner, Frederick Jackson. *The Frontier in American History.* New York: Henry Holt & Company, 1947.

Tuveson, Ernest Lee. *Redeemer Nation: The Idea of America's Millennial Role.* Chicago: University of Chicago Press, 1968.

Updike, John. "Books: Emersonism," in *New Yorker,* June 4, 1984, pp. 112-31.

Van Allmen, Daniel. "The Birth of Theology," in *International Review of Missions,* January 1975.

Vitz, Paul. *Psychology As Religion: The Cult of Self-Worship*. Grand Rapids: Eerdmans, 1977.

Voskuil, Dennis. *Mountains into Goldmines: Robert Schuller and the Gospel of Success*. Grand Rapids: Eerdmans, 1983.

Wacker, Grant. "The Holy Spirit and the Spirit of the Age in American Protestantism, 1880-1910," in *Journal of American History*, 72, 1 (June 1985): 45-62.

Walter, J. A. *A Long Way from Home: A Sociological Exploration of Contemporary Idolatry*. Exeter: Paternoster, 1979.

Weinberg, Albert K. *Manifest Destiny: A Study of Nationalist Expansionism in American History*. Glouchester, MA: Peter Smith, 1958.

White, Patrick. *Voss*. New York: Viking Press, 1957.

White, Ronald C., Jr., and C. Howard Hopkins. *The Social Gospel: Religion and Reform in Changing America*. Philadelphia: Temple University Press, 1976.

White, Ronald C., Jr., Louis B. Weeks, and Garth M. Rosell. *American Christianity: A Case Approach*. Grand Rapids: Eerdmans, 1986.

Williams, Robin M., Jr. *American Society: A Sociological Interpretation*. 2nd edition. New York: Alfred A. Knopf, 1960.

Wills, Garry. *Inventing America: Jefferson's Declaration of Independence*. New York: Doubleday, 1978.

Wood, Gordon S. "Conspiracy and the Paranoid Style: Causality and Deceit in the Eighteenth Century," in *William and Mary Quarterly*, 39, 3 (July 1982): 401-41.

Woodbridge, John D., Mark A. Noll, and Nathan O. Hatch. *The Gospel in America: Themes in the Story of America's Evangelicals*. Grand Rapids: Zondervan, 1979.

Woodward, C. Vann. *The Burden of Southern History*. Baton Rouge: Louisiana State University Press, 1960.

————. "The Fall of the American Adam," in *The New Republic*, December 2, 1981, pp. 13-16.

Yoder, John Howard. "But We Do See Jesus! The Particularity of the Incarnation and the Universality of Truth," in *Foundations of Ethics*. Ed. Leroy S. Rouner. Notre Dame: Notre Dame University Press, 1983.